"This series is a tremendous resource ↑
understanding of how the gospel is w
pastors and scholars doing gospel busi
logical feast preparing God's people to
wholly committed to Christ's priorities.

**BRYAN CHAPELL,** President Emeritus, Covenant Theological Seminary; Senior Pastor, Grace Presbyterian Church, Peoria, Illinois

"Mark Twain may have smiled when he wrote to a friend, 'I didn't have time to write you a short letter, so I wrote you a long letter.' But the truth of Twain's remark remains serious and universal, because well-reasoned, compact writing requires extra time and extra hard work. And this is what we have in the Crossway Bible study series *Knowing the Bible*. The skilled authors and notable editors provide the contours of each book of the Bible as well as the grand theological themes that bind them together as one Book. Here, in a 12-week format, are carefully wrought studies that will ignite the mind and the heart."

**R. KENT HUGHES,** Visiting Professor of Practical Theology, Westminster Theological Seminary

"*Knowing the Bible* brings together a gifted team of Bible teachers to produce a high-quality series of study guides. The coordinated focus of these materials is unique: biblical content, provocative questions, systematic theology, practical application, and the gospel story of God's grace presented all the way through Scripture."

**PHILIP G. RYKEN,** President, Wheaton College

"These *Knowing the Bible* volumes provide a significant and very welcome variation on the general run of inductive Bible studies. This series provides substantial instruction, as well as teaching through the very questions that are asked. *Knowing the Bible* then goes even further by showing how any given text links with the gospel, the whole Bible, and the formation of theology. I heartily endorse this orientation of individual books to the whole Bible and the gospel, and I applaud the demonstration that sound theology was not something invented later by Christians, but is right there in the pages of Scripture."

**GRAEME L. GOLDSWORTHY,** former lecturer, Moore Theological College; author, *According to Plan, Gospel and Kingdom, The Gospel in Revelation,* and *Gospel and Wisdom*

"What a gift to earnest, Bible-loving, Bible-searching believers! The organization and structure of the Bible study format presented through the *Knowing the Bible* series is so well conceived. Students of the Word are led to understand the content of passages through perceptive, guided questions, and they are given rich insights and application all along the way in the brief but illuminating sections that conclude each study. What potential growth in depth and breadth of understanding these studies offer! One can only pray that vast numbers of believers will discover more of God and the beauty of his Word through these rich studies."

**BRUCE A. WARE,** Professor of Christian Theology, The Southern Baptist Theological Seminary

# KNOWING THE BIBLE

J. I. Packer, Theological Editor
Dane C. Ortlund, Series Editor
Lane T. Dennis, Executive Editor

•  •  •  •  •  •

| | | | |
|---|---|---|---|
| Genesis | Psalms | Jonah, Micah, and Nahum | Ephesians |
| Exodus | Proverbs | | Philippians |
| Leviticus | Ecclesiastes | Haggai, Zechariah, and Malachi | Colossians and Philemon |
| Numbers | Song of Solomon | | |
| Deuteronomy | Isaiah | Matthew | 1–2 Thessalonians |
| Joshua | Jeremiah | Mark | 1–2 Timothy and Titus |
| Judges | Lamentations, Habakkuk, and Zephaniah | Luke | |
| Ruth and Esther | | John | Hebrews |
| 1–2 Samuel | | Acts | James |
| 1–2 Kings | Ezekiel | Romans | 1–2 Peter and Jude |
| 1–2 Chronicles | Daniel | 1 Corinthians | |
| Ezra and Nehemiah | Hosea | 2 Corinthians | 1–3 John |
| Job | Joel, Amos, and Obadiah | Galatians | Revelation |

•  •  •  •  •  •

**J. I. PACKER** was the former Board of Governors' Professor of Theology at Regent College (Vancouver, BC). Dr. Packer earned his DPhil at the University of Oxford. He is known and loved worldwide as the author of the best-selling book *Knowing God*, as well as many other titles on theology and the Christian life. He served as the General Editor of the ESV Bible and as the Theological Editor for the *ESV Study Bible*.

**LANE T. DENNIS** is CEO of Crossway, a not-for-profit publishing ministry. Dr. Dennis earned his PhD from Northwestern University. He is Chair of the ESV Bible Translation Oversight Committee and Executive Editor of the *ESV Study Bible*.

**DANE C. ORTLUND** (PhD, Wheaton College) serves as senior pastor of Naperville Presbyterian Church in Naperville, Illinois. He is an editor for the Knowing the Bible series and the Short Studies in Biblical Theology series, and is the author of several books, including *Gentle and Lowly: The Heart of Christ for Sinners and Sufferers*.

# ISAIAH

## A 12-WEEK STUDY

Drew Hunter

WHEATON, ILLINOIS

*Knowing the Bible: Isaiah, A 12-Week Study*

Copyright © 2013 by Crossway

Published by Crossway
        1300 Crescent Street
        Wheaton, Illinois 60187

Some content used in this study guide has been adapted from the *ESV Study Bible*, copyright © 2008 by Crossway, pages 1233–1362. Used by permission. All rights reserved.

Cover design: Simplicated Studio

First printing 2013

Printed in the United States of America

Trade paperback ISBN: 978-1-4335-3434-8
PDF ISBN: 978-1-4335-3435-5
Mobipocket ISBN: 978-1-4335-3436-2
EPub ISBN: 978-1-4335-3437-9

Crossway is a publishing ministry of Good News Publishers.

| VP | | | 31 | 30 | 29 | 28 | 27 | 26 | 25 | 24 |
|----|----|----|----|----|----|----|----|----|----|----|
| 21 | 20 | 19 | 18 | 17 | 16 | 15 | 14 | 13 | 12 | |

# TABLE OF CONTENTS

# SERIES PREFACE

**KNOWING THE BIBLE**, as the series title indicates, was created to help readers know and understand the meaning, the message, and the God of the Bible. Each volume in the series consists of 12 units that progressively take the reader through a clear, concise study of that book of the Bible. In this way, any given volume can fruitfully be used in a 12-week format either in group study, such as in a church-based context, or in individual study. Of course, these 12 studies could be completed in fewer or more than 12 weeks, as convenient, depending on the context in which they are used.

Each study unit gives an overview of the text at hand before digging into it with a series of questions for reflection or discussion. The unit then concludes by highlighting the gospel of grace in each passage ("Gospel Glimpses"), identifying whole-Bible themes that occur in the passage ("Whole-Bible Connections"), and pinpointing Christian doctrines that are affirmed in the passage ("Theological Soundings").

The final component to each unit is a section for reflecting on personal and practical implications from the passage at hand. The layout provides space for recording responses to the questions proposed, and we think readers need to do this to get the full benefit of the exercise. The series also includes definitions of key words. These definitions are indicated by a note number in the text and are found at the end of each chapter.

Lastly, to help understand the Bible in this deeper way, we urge readers to use the ESV Bible and the *ESV Study Bible*, which are available in various print and digital formats, including online editions at esv.org. The Knowing the Bible series is also available online.

May the Lord greatly bless your study as you seek to know him through knowing his Word.

J. I. Packer

Lane T. Dennis

# WEEK 1: OVERVIEW

▲

> ## Getting Acquainted

The Hebrew meaning of Isaiah's name summarizes his message: The Lord saves. The prophecy of Isaiah alternates between promises of judgment and restoration, continually reminding us of the magnitude of humanity's sin, the judgment that all deserve, and the God who displays his glory by saving sinners.

The message is not for Israel and Judah alone, but for the whole world. Isaiah rebukes all nations for their unfaithfulness to God, yet announces a surprising plan of grace and glory for any sinner who comes to him in faith. As we are surprised by grace time and again throughout the book, a glorious picture of God's cosmic renewal develops. Central to this salvation is the sending of a Messiah, a servant-king who will suffer for his people and be exalted in victory.

Isaiah presents God in all his glory, worthy of all our trust. He is the redeemer who rescues from sin and restores all things, to the praise of his glorious grace. (For further background, see the ESV *Study Bible*, pages 1233–1239; available online at esv.org.)

> ## Placing It in the Larger Story

Isaiah stands at a turning point in the history of God's people when, after centuries of breaking their covenant[1] relationship, God's judgment will fall upon them and, indeed, the whole world. Yet Isaiah proclaims the "good news" that God will bring his kingdom, renew all creation, and restore his people to himself. This redemption will be accomplished through a servant, who will suffer in the place of sinners that they might be forgiven and restored to God. Through his life, death, and resurrection, Jesus has begun to fulfill in a decisive way the promises of Isaiah. We await the day when Jesus returns to gather the redeemed to worship God in a new creation forever.

## Key Verse

"And the glory of the LORD shall be revealed, and all flesh shall see it together, for the mouth of the LORD has spoken" (Isa. 40:5).

## Date and Historical Background

Isaiah's writing can be dated within the time frame of his ministry, which began in 740 BC and continued to the 680s. He served when God's people were divided into two kingdoms: the northern kingdom of Israel and the southern kingdom of Judah. Isaiah's ministry was in the context of Judah as their lengthy period of prosperity declined in the shadow of the rising threat of Assyria. Because of their continual rebellion, Judah would eventually be exiled[2] to Babylon.

Isaiah's prophecy assumes three different historical backgrounds: his own context in the eighth century BC (Isaiah 1–39), Israel's exile in Babylon in the sixth century (40–55), and after the exiles have returned to their land (56–66). Yet the entirety of Isaiah's message challenged his own contemporaries and continues to remain relevant to all of God's people until Jesus returns.

## Outline

   I. Introduction: "Ah, Sinful Nation!" (1:1–5:30)

   II. God Redefines the Future of His People: "Your Guilt Is Taken Away" (6:1–12:6)

   III. God's Judgment and Grace for the World: "We Have a Strong City" (13:1–27:13)

   IV. God's Sovereign Word Spoken into the World: "Ah!" (28:1–35:10)

   V. Historical Transition: "In Whom Do You Now Trust?" (36:1–39:8)

   VI. Comfort for God's Exiles: "The Glory of the Lord Shall Be Revealed" (40:1–55:13)

   VII. How to Prepare for the Coming Glory: "Hold Fast My Covenant" (56:1–66:24)

## As You Get Started

What is your understanding of how Isaiah helps us to grasp the whole story line of the Bible? Do you have an idea of how aspects of Isaiah's message are fulfilled in the New Testament?

What is your current understanding of what Isaiah contributes to Christian theology? How does his book clarify our understanding of God, Jesus Christ, sin, salvation, the end times, or any other doctrine?

What aspects of the prophecy of Isaiah have confused you? Are there any specific questions that you hope to have answered through this study?

## As You Finish This Unit . . .

Take a few minutes to ask God to bless you with increased understanding and a transformed heart and life as you begin this study of Isaiah.

### Definitions

[1] **Covenant** – A binding agreement between two parties, typically involving a formal statement of their relationship, a list of stipulations and obligations for both parties, a list of witnesses to the agreement, and a list of curses for unfaithfulness and blessings for faithfulness to the agreement.

[2] **Exile** – Several relocations of large groups of Israelites/Jews have occurred throughout history, but "the exile" typically refers to the Babylonian exile, that is, Nebuchadnezzar's relocation of residents of the southern kingdom of Judah to Babylon in 586 BC (residents of the northern kingdom of Israel had been resettled by Assyria in 722 BC). After Babylon came under Persian rule, several waves of Jewish exiles returned and repopulated Judah.

# WEEK 2:
# CONFRONTATION
# AND HOPE FOR
# GOD'S PEOPLE

Isaiah 1:1–5:30

▲

This first section introduces the book and, in doing so, introduces the problem God addresses through the prophet Isaiah. "Children have I reared and brought up," God says, "but they have rebelled against me" (Isa. 1:2). The people who were supposed to be a holy nation are a "sinful nation" (1:4). Even as Judah's sin is thoroughly confronted, this first section also gives us a glimpse of God's purposes to bring grace for his people and, indeed, for the whole world.

Isaiah 1–5 shows us the depth of Judah's sinfulness, the judgment they deserve, and the grace that God promises to bring to them and the rest of the world.

> ## Reflection and Discussion

Read through the complete passage for this study, Isaiah 1–5. Then review the questions below and write your notes on them concerning this introductory section to Isaiah's prophecy. (For further background, see the *ESV Study Bible*, pages 1240–1250; also available online at esv.org.)

### 1. God's Confrontation of Judah's Sin (1:1–30)

As the heavens and earth are called into the courtroom as witnesses, God announces the charge against his people (Isa. 1:2–6). What are they accused of? Referring to Judah as "children" or "sons" of God highlights their great privilege (v. 2). It also points to God's patience, for he graciously endured their rebellion from the time he first called them his "son" at the exodus[1] (Ex. 4:22–23; Deut. 14:1). How does this help us to see the great offense of Israel's ongoing problem?

"What to me is the multitude of your sacrifices? . . . I do not delight in the blood of bulls, or of lambs, or of goats" (Isa. 1:11). At first glance, it appears God is rejecting the very acts of worship he previously required of his people in Leviticus. Yet 1:10–20 shows it is hypocrisy, not worship, that God opposes. The ordinances were always intended to foster true godliness, which would be demonstrated in humble purity of heart and energetic promotion of others' well-being. According to verses 13–17, how did Israel divorce these worship practices from their original purposes? In what ways is religious hypocrisy seen today?

"How the faithful city has become a whore" (Isa. 1:21). The covenant God made with Israel after the exodus was viewed as a marriage covenant (54:5). Why does Isaiah use such shocking language here? What does this tell us about the way God views sin?

## 2. God's Promises of Judgment and Grace (2:1–4:6)

From their first appearance in Genesis 49:1 onward, phrases such as "in the latter days" (Isa. 2:2) are often used in contexts charged with end-time expectations, typically connected to the establishment of God's kingdom and the redemption of his people (Gen. 49:1, 10; Num. 24:14–19; Deut. 4:30–31; Dan. 2:28–35; Hos. 3:5). The focus here is on a future exaltation of the Temple Mount in Jerusalem. Since gods in the ancient Near East were thought to dwell at the heights of mountains, what is Isaiah communicating by insisting on the exaltation of God's dwelling place over all? What results of this exaltation appear in Isaiah 2:1–5?

"For you have rejected your people . . . " This begins the lengthy section announcing God's approaching judgment against his people's rebellion (Isa. 2:6–4:1). Review 2:8, 17–18; 3:8, 14–16 (note also 1:21–23). What has Israel done to deserve judgment? Since we can learn what God is *for* by hearing what he is *against*, what does this section teach us about God?

13

How is Isaiah 2:22 a fitting command in light of the promise of a day when "the lofty pride of men shall be brought low, and the LORD alone will be exalted" (v. 17)?

_____

_____

_____

_____

_____

_____

We saw the numerous reasons for Israel's condemnation in Isaiah 2–3. Yet in a surprising entrance of grace, God promises to provide "the branch of the LORD," the Messiah[2] (4:2). Read Jeremiah 23:5–6; 33:15; Zechariah 3:8–9; 6:12–13. Who is "the Branch," and what else will he do?

_____

_____

_____

_____

_____

_____

### 3. God's Condemnation of Judah's Sin (5:1–30)

Israel was God's "pleasant planting" and carefully cultivated vineyard (Isa. 5:7). Yet as Isaiah sings about this vineyard in 5:1–7, we learn that they failed to produce the fruit of righteousness that God expected. They brought forth only unwanted "wild grapes" (v. 4). In 5:8–30 a cycle of six "woes" shows us some of these bitter fruits of Israel's degenerate character. What are they?

_____

_____

_____

_____

_____

_____

This section ends with a terrifying scene (Isa. 5:26–30). The sovereign God will summon nations, including Assyria, to carry out his judgment against his people. There only remains a picture of "de-creation,"[3] darkness, and chaos (v. 30). What have we already seen about God's character and promises in chapters 1–4 that gives assurance that there is still hope?

_____

_____

_____

_____

_____

_____

_____

_____

Read through the following three sections on *Gospel Glimpses, Whole-Bible Connections*, and *Theological Soundings*. Then take time to consider the *Personal Implications* these sections may have for you.

## ▶ Gospel Glimpses

**INVITATION.** When Adam and Eve rebelled against God in Eden, they were sent away from his presence. As their descendants, we're all born outside of God's presence and continue to rebel against him. Yet God invites us back. Even after Israel provoked God with their many sins, he still extended an invitation of grace: "Come now, let us reason together, says the LORD: though your sins are like scarlet, they shall be as white as snow" (Isa. 1:18). It is ultimately the blood of Jesus that cleanses us in this way (1 John 1:7). He invites us to "Come to me, all who labor and are heavy laden, and I will give you rest" (Matt. 11:28).

**SURPRISING GRACE.** Throughout Isaiah 2:6–4:1, we hear what God will do "in that day"—a day of utter terror for sinners (2:20–21). In 4:2 Isaiah once again says, "in that day," only this time it is followed by an unexpected, surging wave of grace. Isaiah often introduces grace as a surprise. In this instance, God promises to provide "the branch of the LORD," the Messiah (4:2). His people will be washed of their filth (4:3–4) and the presence of the God they defied will become their refuge (4:5–6; note 3:8). God's surprising grace to sinners should never get old. The New Testament words, "But God," should always awaken fresh wonder. "And you were dead in the trespasses . . . *But God* . . . made us alive together with Christ—by *grace* you have been saved" (Eph. 2:1, 4–5).

15

## Whole-Bible Connections

**GOD'S FAITHFUL CITY AND BRIDE.** Because Israel rejected God, "the faithful city has become a whore" (Isa. 1:21). They are like a faithful city that has become faithless, and a bride who abandoned her marriage covenant. Yet Isaiah looks to the future and sees restoration: "Afterward you shall be called the city of righteousness, the faithful city" (1:26). She will be a faithful city and bride because of Jesus Christ, who loved her and gave himself up for her on the cross (Eph. 5:25). Revelation describes the ultimate fulfillment of Isaiah's promise: "I saw the holy city, new Jerusalem, coming down out of heaven from God, prepared as a bride adorned for her husband" (Rev. 21:2; note also vv. 10–11).

**THE TRUE VINE.** "Let me sing for my beloved my love song concerning his vineyard" (Isa. 5:1). Using the metaphor of a vineyard, Isaiah's song retells Israel's history from their initial "planting" in Canaan to their continual failure to bear righteous fruit (5:1–7). While Isaiah sees destruction coming in the future (5:5–6), the psalmist later writes from the midst of it and pleads for God to "have regard for this vine" (Ps. 80:14). This is the background to Jesus' announcement, "I am the *true* vine" (John 15:1). He is the True Vine who bore the fruit of righteousness that Israel and all of us failed to produce. Although he is the only one who didn't deserve to be destroyed like the unfruitful vine of Isaiah 5, Jesus took this destruction in our place on the cross. And now, through faith in him, any failed vine can be united to the True Vine and begin to bear good fruit. "Whoever abides in me and I in him, he it is that bears much fruit" (John 15:5).

## Theological Soundings

**THE WORD OF GOD.** This book is "the vision of Isaiah" (Isa. 1:1). As a prophet who receives a vision, Isaiah is called to declare God's word to his world. Thus, when Isaiah speaks, it is no contradiction to say, "the LORD has spoken" (v. 2), and "hear the word of the LORD" (v. 10). Like others who wrote Scripture, Isaiah "spoke from God as [he was] carried along by the Holy Spirit" (2 Pet. 1:21; see also 2 Tim. 3:16). As we read Isaiah's words, we are reading the very words of God.

**THE DEPTHS OF SIN.** The book of Isaiah is unrelenting in its confrontation of sin. From the beginning, we see that God's people have rebelled (Isa. 1:2) and are a "sinful nation, a people laden with iniquity, offspring of evildoers, children who deal corruptly" (v. 4). What is worse, they sin against grace, for God cared for them as his children (1:2; 5:4). Since we are corrupt in every part of our being, God's redemption must (and does) include comprehensive cleansing and renewal.

## Personal Implications

Take time to reflect on the implications of Isaiah 1–5 for your own life today. Consider what you have learned that might lead you to praise God, repent of sin, and trust in his gracious promises. Make notes below on the personal implications for your walk with the Lord of (1) the *Gospel Glimpses*, (2) the *Whole-Bible Connections*, (3) the *Theological Soundings*, and (4) this passage as a whole.

### 1. Gospel Glimpses

### 2. Whole-Bible Connections

### 3. Theological Soundings

## 4. Isaiah 1–5

---

---

---

---

---

---

---

---

## As You Finish This Unit . . .

Take a moment now to ask for the Lord's blessing and help as you continue in this study of Isaiah. And take a moment also to look back through this unit of study, to reflect on some key things that the Lord may be teaching you—and perhaps to highlight and underline these things to review again in the future.

### Definitions

[1] **The exodus** – The departure of the people of Israel from Egypt and their journey to Mount Sinai under Moses' leadership (Exodus 1–19; Numbers 33).

[2] **Messiah** – A transliteration of a Hebrew word meaning "anointed one," the equivalent of the Greek word Christ. Originally applied to anyone specially designated for a particular role, such as king or priest. Jesus himself affirmed that he was the Messiah sent from God (Matt. 16:16–17).

[3] **De-creation** – The reversal of the goodness and blessing of God's creation. As the blessing of creation is described as light out of darkness, order from chaos, and filling emptiness (Gen. 1:1–2:3), judgment is sometimes described as a return to darkness, chaos, and emptiness (Jer. 4:23–26).

# WEEK 3:
# SALVATION THROUGH
# JUDGMENT FOR
# GOD'S PEOPLE

Isaiah 6:1–12:6

## The Place of the Passage

After the sober introduction to Israel's sinfulness and the promised judgment and grace to come, chapter 6 introduces us to Isaiah and his commission to proclaim God's message. While judgment will certainly fall upon unfaithful Judah and Israel, God's grace will preserve a remnant to be restored and enjoy his salvation. This grace begins with Isaiah (Isa. 6:1–13) and will spread to the remnant of God's people (7:1–11:16), leading them to a day of worldwide praise (12:1–6).

## The Big Picture

In Isaiah 6–12, we see God's grace extended to Isaiah, then promised to the southern kingdom of Judah and the northern kingdom of Israel.

> ## Reflection and Discussion

Read through the entire text for this study, Isaiah 6–12. Then interact with the following questions and record your notes on them concerning this section of Isaiah's prophecy. (For further background, see the *ESV Study Bible*, pages 1251–1264; also available online at esv.org.)

### 1. The Triumph of Grace for Isaiah (6:1–13)

God's holiness implies his absolute moral purity and separateness above creation. What are several ways Isaiah 6:1–5 demonstrates this?

Isaiah's sin is atoned[1] for through the sacrifice on the altar, and he is subsequently restored to God and commissioned to proclaim his message (vv. 6–10). How would Isaiah's experience provide hope for God's people in light of their desperate situation described in chapters 1–5? How might it do the same for us?

God decrees that Isaiah's ministry will harden his own sinful generation (Isa. 6:9–10). God's discipline will leave only a remnant[2] of his people, like a stump after a forest fire. Yet this stump will be a "holy seed," a remnant saved by grace (6:13). How would this encourage Isaiah as he preaches this message of hardening? How does all of this relate to proclaiming the gospel in the New Testament (note Matt. 13:13–16; Acts 28:26–28)?

## 2. The Triumph of Grace for Judah and Israel (7:1–11:16)

At this point in history, God's people are divided into two kingdoms, Israel in the north and Judah in the south. Syria and Israel (called "Ephraim" here) come together to force Judah into their alliance against Assyria (Isa. 7:1–2). What would Ahaz, the king of Judah, be tempted to do? Why? In contrast, what is he called to do?

In response to Ahaz's hypocritical refusal to request a sign, God offers the southern kingdom of Judah the sign of a child called "Immanuel," which means "God with us" (Isa. 7:10–14). What is the message of this sign in its original context (note vv. 14–17)? Is it a threat, a promise, or somehow both? Christian interpretation follows Matthew in seeing this as fully and finally fulfilled in the person of Jesus Christ, who is literally "God with us" (Matt. 1:23).

The Assyrian army will eventually destroy Syria, the northern kingdom of Israel, and even the southern kingdom of Judah for their unbelief (Isa. 7:18–8:8). God calls Isaiah and a faithful remnant "not to walk in the way of this people" (8:11). According to 8:11–17, how are they to be characterized?

After the darkness of judgment, the light of grace will dawn (Isa. 9:1–7). Israel will be filled with joy because "a child is born . . . a son is given" (v. 6). What do the four "titles" of this son in verse 6 tell us about who he is and what he will do?

--------

--------

--------

--------

--------

After using Assyria to judge the northern kingdom of Israel (Isa. 9:8–10:4), God will then turn to judge Assyria as well (10:5–19). Why? What does this teach us about God's character?

--------

--------

--------

--------

--------

Isaiah 11:1–10 describes the triumph of the Messiah and the resulting cosmic renewal. Since Jesse was the father of King David, the reference to the Messiah as a "shoot from the stump of Jesse" identifies him as the anticipated Davidic King (v. 1; see Ezek. 34:23–24; 37:24–25; Hos. 3:5). How is he described in verses 2–5? How does this contrast with the character of Israel and any other human? Note a few specific ways this description finds its fulfillment in Jesus Christ.

--------

--------

--------

--------

Read Genesis 1:28–2:3; 3:15. In what ways does Isaiah 11:6–10 imply that the curse will be reversed and Edenic conditions restored?

--------

--------

--------

--------

--------

## 3. The Enjoyment of God and His Grace (12:1–6)

Read Isaiah 12:1–2 with the context of chapters 6–11 in mind. How is the exulting praise of 12:1–2 fitting in light of this?

How is it also fitting that those who have received this grace would take up the missionary call to "let this be made known in all the earth" (v. 5)? What does this imply about the connection between receiving grace and desiring to share it with others (see also Isa. 6:7–8; 2 Cor. 5:14; 1 Pet. 2:9)?

Read through the following three sections on *Gospel Glimpses*, *Whole-Bible Connections*, and *Theological Soundings*. Then take time to consider the *Personal Implications* these sections may have for you.

## Gospel Glimpses

**GUILT REMOVED.** Isaiah knows that nothing unclean can remain in God's holy presence (Hab. 1:13). Having "unclean lips," he rightly cries out, "Woe is me! For I am lost" (6:5). Yet the seraph approaches the sacrifice slain for sinners, grabs a coal, and touches Isaiah's unclean lips with it. "Your guilt is taken away, and your sin atoned for" (v. 7). Rather than take away his life, God took away his guilt. Because of Jesus Christ, the true sacrifice, God offers this same cleansing grace to sinners like Isaiah, including ourselves.

**THE DEPTHS OF JOY.** "With joy you will draw water from the wells of salvation" (Isa. 12:3). Though the depth of our sin runs deep, the depth of God's grace runs deeper. God's people deserve to hear the refrain of chapter 9, "for all this his anger has not turned away, and his hand is stretched out [in judgment] still" (9:12, 17, 21; 10:4). Yet because of his redeeming grace, we say, "though you were angry with me, your anger turned away, that you might comfort me" (12:1). This salvation is a well of joy from which we are daily invited to draw.

## Whole-Bible Connections

**REMNANT.** A remnant of God's people will remain after judgment. In one sense, this is bad news, for *only* a remnant of God's people will be saved: "though your people Israel be as the sand of the sea, only a remnant of them will return" (Isa. 10:22). Yet when no one deserves to survive, the promise of even a remnant is a wonderful encouragement. A remnant chosen by God and saved by grace is a theme that runs throughout the Bible. When God judged the earth with a flood, he saved Noah's family through the ark (Gen. 6:17–18). In the time of Elijah God kept seven thousand from committing idolatry (1 Kings 19:18). When the prophets looked forward to God's salvation after exile, their hope was that a faithful remnant would be saved (Mic. 4:6–7; Zeph. 3:12). When Christ came, he began to gather this remnant to himself. When he returns, he will gather his scattered, now multi-ethnic people, to himself.

**THE DAVIDIC KING.** In Genesis 1:28 we learn that humanity was entrusted with the royal task of "subduing" and "having dominion" over all creation. After Adam, our first king, failed in this calling, God promised that a true and better king would come to conquer evil and restore humanity's rule over the earth. To Abraham and Sarah, God promised, "kings shall come from you" (Gen. 17:6, 16). This promise was narrowed to Judah's line (Gen. 49:10) and, eventually, to the line of David (2 Sam. 7:12–16). The hope is sustained with the promise of a son who will rule "on the throne of David and over his kingdom" (Isa. 9:6–7). This points forward to the coming of Jesus, the son of David, who is now enthroned "far above all rule and authority" (Eph. 1:20–21) and who "shall reign forever and ever" (Rev. 11:15).

## Theological Soundings

**GOD'S HOLINESS.** God confronted Isaiah with a vision of his holiness. Isaiah saw the Lord enthroned as the divine King, "high and lifted up" (Isa. 6:1). In his presence are seraphim, who cause the very threshold of the temple to quake as they declare, "Holy, holy, holy is the LORD of hosts" (v. 3). The Hebrew language uses repetition to communicate the superlative nature of something. Thus, the threefold repetition of "holy" declares God to be utterly unique and supreme in his moral excellence and greatness. God is truly "the Holy One of Israel," a phrase rarely found elsewhere in the Old Testament, yet repeated twenty-five times by Isaiah. The God of the Bible, supremely revealed in Jesus Christ, is pure and righteous, totally "other." He is holy. There is no one like him.

**CHRISTOLOGY.** In Isaiah 6:1–4, Isaiah sees a picture of God exalted as the eternal King, "high and lifted up" (6:1). Isaiah later uses this phrase, "high and lifted up," to describe the suffering servant who will remove the guilt of God's people by his sacrifice (52:13). In the New Testament, John 12:38–41 brings these two references together, applying both to Jesus Christ. This affirms the divinity and humanity of Jesus. He is the exalted Lord and the lowly servant.

**DIVINE SOVEREIGNTY AND HUMAN RESPONSIBILITY.** "Ah, Assyria, the rod of my anger" (Isa. 10:5). When Assyria flooded into Canaan to destroy Israel, it was ultimately God who "sent" them and wielded them like an axe (vv. 6, 15). Then, after using Assyria to judge Israel, God will turn to punish them for their own sins (v. 12), for they arrogantly boasted as though the strength to defeat Israel were their own (vv. 13–15). This text holds together the twin truths of God's sovereignty and human responsibility. In one and the same event, God was sovereign and Assyria was held responsible. God's motives in judging Israel were pure and righteous; Assyria's were arrogant and wicked. While Assyria meant it for evil, God meant it for good (see Gen. 50:20).

## Personal Implications

Take time to reflect on the implications of Isaiah 6–12 for your own life today. Consider what you have learned that might lead you to praise God, repent of sin, and trust in his gracious promises. Make notes below on the personal implications for your walk with the Lord of (1) the *Gospel Glimpses*, (2) the *Whole-Bible Connections*, (3) the *Theological Soundings*, and (4) this passage as a whole.

## 1. Gospel Glimpses

## 2. Whole-Bible Connections

## 3. Theological Soundings

## 4. Isaiah 6–12

### As You Finish This Unit . . .

Take a moment now to ask for the Lord's blessing and help as you continue in this study of Isaiah. And take a moment also to look back through this unit of study, to reflect on key things that the Lord may be teaching you—and perhaps to highlight and underline these things to review again in the future.

### Definitions

[1] **Atonement** – The reconciliation of a person with God, often associated with the offering of a sacrifice. Through his death and resurrection, Jesus Christ made atonement for the sins of believers. His death satisfied God's just wrath against sinful humanity, just as OT sacrifices symbolized substitutionary death as payment for sin.

[2] **Remnant** – In the Bible, a portion of people who remain after most others are destroyed by some catastrophe. The notion of a "remnant" can be found in various events recorded in Scripture, including the flood (Genesis 6–9) and the return of exiled Judah (Ezra 9).

# WEEK 4: SALVATION AND GRACE FOR THE WORLD

Isaiah 13:1–23:18

▲

## The Place of the Passage

The preceding chapters showed God's judgment and grace for God's people, Israel and Judah (Isaiah 6–12). Even there we saw hints of the global purposes of God (9:7; 11:7–9). Now in Isaiah 13–23 the nations become the primary focus. Israel needs to learn that their God, "the Holy One of Israel," is also the Judge and Savior who rules the world. Only he is worthy of their trust. This section progresses with two series of judgment oracles.[1]

## The Big Picture

Isaiah 13–23 shows us that God is the sovereign king, who judges all nations and moves all of history along according to his gracious purposes.

## ▶ Reflection and Discussion

**Read through the complete passage for this study, Isaiah 13–23. Then review the questions below and write your notes on them concerning these two cycles of judgment and grace for the nations. (For further background, see the *ESV Study Bible*, pages 1264–1281; also available online at esv.org.)**

### 1. First Series of Oracles (13:1–20:6)

This section in Isaiah is a string of judgment oracles concerning nations of the world. Yet it is not written *to* those nations; it is written *to* Judah *about* those nations. What is Isaiah helping Judah to see? As you consider this, remember that they were prone to trust in these nations and their false gods rather than the one true God.

Isaiah refers to the coming judgment on Babylon and the nations as "the day of the LORD" (Isa. 13:6, 9). According to Isaiah 13:6–13, what will this "day" be like and why will it occur?

"How you are fallen from heaven, O Day Star, son of Dawn!" (Isa. 14:12). Poetic imagery is used to describe the fall of Babylon's king from the heights of pride to the depths of destruction. Some interpreters also see this as an allusion to the fall of Satan. It also reminds us of humanity's first sin (Gen. 3:5–6). What do vv. 12–15 teach us about the nature of pride? What does this teach us about the end of the arrogant who do not humbly take refuge in Christ?

Babylon will disappear in judgment as though swept away with a broom. Compare this judgment on Babylon (Isa. 14:22–23) with God's judgment on Israel (see especially 10:20–22). How does the extent of judgment differ?

Assyria was the great threat to Israel and Judah in Isaiah's time. While Assyria's downfall is announced in Isaiah 14:24–27, the focus is on "the LORD of hosts." What do we learn about God? How would this message bolster the faith of God's people under the threat of Assyria?

The message of Moab's judgment is in the form of a lament, for it is filled with sorrow (Isa. 15:1–16:14). Moab weeps and prays at their places of worship, the high places[2] (15:2; 16:12). By referring to their "high places," what does Isaiah indicate about their worship (note 2 Kings 17:29; Ps. 78:58)? How does this explain why God ignores their prayers (16:12–14)? What does this show us about religious zeal that is not directed toward the one true God?

Read Deuteronomy 6:10–19. What light does this shed on the condemnation of the northern kingdom of Israel, here referred to as Ephraim (Isa. 17:4–14)? Note, in particular, Isaiah 17:10.

"Striking and healing," God proclaims judgment against Egypt (Isa. 19:1–15) and then restoration for Egypt and the nations (19:16–25). This points forward to the day when those "from every tribe and language and people and nation" will worship God because of the saving work of Christ (Rev. 5:9). What are the various ways that nations will be blessed, according to Isaiah 19:18–25?

## 2. Second Series of Oracles (21:1–23:18)

Isaiah gives us a glimpse of Judah's deep heart-orientation towards self-salvation in the oracle concerning Jerusalem, "the valley of vision" (Isa. 22:1–25). When faced with destruction, Judah looked with great attentiveness to military readiness (vv. 8–11). Yet they should have looked to "him who did it . . .

him who planned it long ago" (v. 11; also 31:1). Why was it foolish for them to "look" away from God? In contrast, what would it mean to "look to" God here?

---

The final oracle is against Tyre, a hub of commerce (Isa. 23:1–18). This city is called a prostitute because money was the driving motive for everything (vv. 15–17). How would this seduction of security and prestige have weakened Judah's trust in God? What are ways that wealth provides a false sense of security or glory? How should God's judgment against Tyre change Judah's perspective (and our own) toward such people and nations?

---

Read through the following three sections on *Gospel Glimpses*, *Whole-Bible Connections*, and *Theological Soundings*. Then take time to consider the *Personal Implications* these sections may have for you.

## Gospel Glimpses

**LOOKING TO OUR MAKER.** "In that day man will look to his Maker. . . . He will not look to the altars, the work of his hands" (Isa. 17:7–8). All efforts of false religion are, at bottom, self-salvation projects. In utter self-reliance, we offer the work of our hands to gain the approval and acceptance of God and others. But with his final words on the cross, "It is finished," Jesus announced the accomplishment of our salvation. We must look away from our bad works and also our good works and look only to Christ and his finished work.

**THE REACH OF GRACE.** From the early chapters of Exodus, we learn that the Egyptians were enemies of God and oppressors of Israel. But when "the people of Israel groaned because of their slavery and cried out for help," God delivered them (Ex. 2:23–24). Egypt, of course, rightly deserves to be judged. Yet God's grace will extend even to them, and in a strikingly similar manner as it did to Israel. "When they cry to the Lord because of oppressors, he will send them a savior and defender, and deliver them" (Isa. 19:20–21). No one is beyond the reach of God's grace.

**COMPASSION.** In the midst of words of judgment against the nations we find words of comfort for Israel: "For the Lord will have compassion on Jacob and will again choose Israel" (14:1). God is righteous and just. Thus, he is rightly provoked to wrath by the prideful rebellion of Israel, the nations, and every one of us. Yet he sets his heart in love on his people and overflows with compassion toward us. Not an ounce of that love is deserved.

## Whole-Bible Connections

**BABYLON.** We gain insight into the prideful character of Babylon as Genesis 11:1–9 describes the nation's beginning: "let us build ourselves a city and a tower with its top in the heavens, and let us make a name for ourselves" (Gen. 11:4). As the story line of Scripture progresses, Babylon becomes a symbol for all prideful rebellion against God. We learn from Isaiah that Babylon is marked by such arrogance (13:11) and will, therefore, be judged (13:1–22; 21:1–10). Yet even after destruction, the haughty spirit of Babylon lives on in the mighty nations of the world. Peter, for instance, refers to Rome as "Babylon" (1 Pet. 5:13). John, too, announces the ultimate downfall of prideful world powers with the words from Isaiah, "Fallen, fallen is Babylon" (Rev. 18:2; Isa. 21:9).

**THE DAY OF THE LORD.** Isaiah twice referred to "the day of the Lord" in the oracle concerning Babylon (Isa. 13:6, 9). For Babylon, this day will be "cruel, with wrath and fierce anger" (13:9). The prophets often use this phrase to refer to a future time of judgment. It is a "day of vengeance" for the Lord to "avenge himself on his foes" (Jer. 46:10; also Ezek. 30:3; Joel 1:15; 2:1, 11; Amos 5:18–20; Obad. 15; Zeph. 1:7, 14; Mal. 4:5). This "day" is not limited to one particular date on the calendar, for at one level it has occurred on several occasions throughout the Old Testament. According to 2 Peter 3:10–13, however, there will be an ultimate fulfillment in the future, when Jesus returns to judge the world and establish the new heavens and new earth.

## Theological Soundings

**UNIVERSAL JUDGMENT.** This section of Isaiah draws our attention to God's judgment against several nations, representative of the whole world. Indeed,

God declares, "I will punish the world for its evil" (Isa. 13:11). God will bring a universal judgment over all nations. Jesus, who has received all authority from his Father, will carry out this judgment. God "has fixed a day on which he will judge the world in righteousness by a man [Jesus] whom he has appointed" (Acts 17:31).

**DIVINE SORROW.** The Moabites wept because of the judgment proclaimed against them (Isa. 15:1–16:14). But they are not the only ones weeping. The sovereign King, who is judging in righteousness, also weeps. "My heart cries out for Moab," God says, "I drench you with my tears" (15:5; 16:9). He is a righteous judge, committed to removing all prideful rebellion against his rule. Yet his is a judgment mixed with grief, for he asks, "Have I any pleasure in the death of the wicked, declares the Lord GOD, and not rather that he should turn from his way and live?" (Ezek. 18:23).

## Personal Implications

Take time to reflect on the implications of Isaiah 13–23 for your own life today. Consider what you have learned that might lead you to praise God, repent of sin, and trust in his gracious promises. Make notes below on the personal implications for your walk with the Lord of (1) the *Gospel Glimpses*, (2) the *Whole-Bible Connections*, (3) the *Theological Soundings*, and (4) this passage as a whole.

## 1. Gospel Glimpses

## 2. Whole-Bible Connections

## 3. Theological Soundings

_____

_____

_____

_____

_____

_____

## 4. Isaiah 13–23

_____

_____

_____

_____

_____

_____

> ### As You Finish This Unit . . .

Take a moment now to ask for the Lord's blessing and help as you continue in this study of Isaiah. And take a moment also to look back through this unit of study, to reflect on some key things that the Lord may be teaching you—and perhaps to highlight and underline these things to review again in the future.

### Definitions

[1] **Oracle** – From Latin "to speak." In the Bible, refers to a divine pronouncement delivered through a human agent.

[2] **High places** – Height may or may not have been a feature of these public sites where offerings were made to God or to false gods. Worshipping the Lord at a high place was legitimate before the time of the temple (1 Kings 3:2, 4). Later "high places," even those where the Lord was worshiped, were forbidden (2 Kings 23:15).

# WEEK 5:
# THE FINAL END

Isaiah 24:1–27:13

## The Place of the Passage

Two cycles of judgment oracles lead up to this point, each of which addressed particular nations (Isaiah 13–20; 21–23). Now in chapters 24–27, we come to the climax of God's message of judgment and salvation for the whole world. The wicked will be condemned and God's people will be lavishly blessed. These four chapters are often called "apocalyptic"[1] because of the imagery used to depict God's final victory.

## The Big Picture

Isaiah 24–27 describes the end of this present age, when God judges the nations and saves his people.

> ### Reflection and Discussion

Read through the complete passage for this study, Isaiah 24–27. Then review the questions below and write your notes on them concerning this section to Isaiah's prophecy. (For further background, see the *ESV Study Bible*, pages 1281–1287; also available online at esv.org.)

### 1. The Wasted City and the Global Feast (24:1–25:12)

Isaiah 24:1–20 describes the violent dismantling of this present age and its replacement with joyous worldwide worship. The people have rejected God's revealed will in order to construct their own alternative social order. This sin (v. 5) leads to a curse (v. 6). Where else in the Old Testament have we seen this pattern? What are the effects of this curse (vv. 6–13)?

--------------------------------------------------------------

--------------------------------------------------------------

--------------------------------------------------------------

With the mention of "on that day" in Isaiah 24:21 and throughout chapters 24–27 (25:9; 26:1; 27:1, 2, 12, 13), we are alerted that the time frame under discussion is the same as 24:1–20, namely, the focal point toward which God is leading history. God will reign as king and will display his glory to the leaders of his people, just as he did when he made the first covenant with Israel (24:23; see Ex. 24:9–11). Why do the moon and sun seem to hang their heads in shame? Consider what light Isaiah 60:19–20 sheds on the answer (also Rev. 21:23; 22:4–5).

--------------------------------------------------------------

--------------------------------------------------------------

--------------------------------------------------------------

--------------------------------------------------------------

After overthrowing human tyranny (Isa. 25:1–5), God will spread a banquet for his people (v. 6; see 24:23). Note how Revelation draws on the promises of verses 6–9 to give hope to God's people (Rev. 19:7–9; 21:3–4; also 1 Cor. 15:54). What do the descriptions of the food and wine indicate about the way God blesses? What does the repetition of "all" in vv. 6–9 indicate? In light of Isaiah 55:1–3, who is invited to the feast and how much will it cost?

## 2. Singing in the Secure City (26:1–21)

The city is an important image in Isaiah 24–27 (see 24:10, 12; 25:2; 26:1–2, 5; 27:10). Isaiah views the entire world culture as a "lofty city" (26:5) because it is a place of imagined safety and prideful self-sufficiency. But God will destroy it and establish a "strong city" for his people. What is the primary characteristic of those who will be in God's city (26:1–4; see also 7:9; 12:2; 30:15)? What are specific ways that the mind-set of the "lofty city" is seen today, and how are we tempted to embrace it?

Isaiah 26 records Israel's song of praise to God in light of his coming triumph. Yet they sing as those who have not yet received all of God's blessings. They wait, even in the midst of distress (vv.16–18, 20–21). What does this chapter show us about the heart of God's people (note especially vv. 7–9; see also Ps. 63:1–8; 73:23–28; Phil. 1:21–23; 3:7–11)? How is this attitude significant in light of their circumstances?

In Isaiah 26:20–21, God graciously invites his people to hide inside while he punishes the world for their sin. Where else have we seen something similar? For help, see Genesis 7:1–7, 15–16 and Exodus 12:21–23. Are there any specific ways that Isaiah alludes to these texts?

-------------------------------------------------------------------------
-------------------------------------------------------------------------
-------------------------------------------------------------------------
-------------------------------------------------------------------------
-------------------------------------------------------------------------
-------------------------------------------------------------------------

### 3. The Redemption of God's People (27:1–13)

What are the specific ways in which the vineyard story of Isaiah 27:2–5 is similar to that of 5:1–7? How is it different? How does this description remind us of Eden before the curse (Genesis 1–3)?

-------------------------------------------------------------------------
-------------------------------------------------------------------------
-------------------------------------------------------------------------
-------------------------------------------------------------------------
-------------------------------------------------------------------------
-------------------------------------------------------------------------

The Jubilee year was announced with the blowing of the trumpet on the Day of Atonement.[2] Read the description of this in Leviticus 25:8–12. What does Isaiah 27:13 say will happen when this trumpet sounds in the future? How does this help us understand what the New Testament authors mean in texts such as Matthew 24:31 and 1 Thessalonians 4:16 (also 1 Cor. 15:52)?

-------------------------------------------------------------------------
-------------------------------------------------------------------------
-------------------------------------------------------------------------
-------------------------------------------------------------------------
-------------------------------------------------------------------------
-------------------------------------------------------------------------

Looking back over these chapters, we see that God's people are filled with songs of praise. Review Isaiah 24:14–16; 25:1–5, 9–10; and 26:1–5. Why, specifically, do they praise God? With what titles do they refer to him, and what do these indicate about him?

--------------------------------------------------------------------------------

--------------------------------------------------------------------------------

--------------------------------------------------------------------------------

--------------------------------------------------------------------------------

--------------------------------------------------------------------------------

--------------------------------------------------------------------------------

Read through the following three sections on *Gospel Glimpses, Whole-Bible Connections*, and *Theological Soundings*. Then take time to consider the *Personal Implications* these sections may have for you.

## ▶ Gospel Glimpses

**CAUSE FOR PRAISE.** "Behold, this is our God; we have waited for him, that he might save us. . . . let us be glad and rejoice in his salvation" (Isa. 25:9). The text does not say, "we have *worked* for him, that he might save us." That would leave us with cause for pride, not cause for praise. God is the one, fundamentally, who works. We are the ones who wait. Salvation is accomplished according to God's plan, at his initiative, and through his saving work in Christ. We simply trust him to save, and rejoice that he does.

**REFUGE FROM WRATH.** "Come, my people, enter your chambers, and shut your doors behind you; hide yourselves for a little while until the fury has passed by" (Isa. 26:20). Although God is going to "punish the inhabitants of the earth for their iniquity" (v. 21), he invites his people to a place of refuge. He has done this before. When he judged the earth with a flood, Noah's family took refuge in the ark. When he destroyed the firstborn in Egypt, Israel took refuge behind blood-smeared doors. He now invites all to take refuge in his Son, who sheltered us from God's wrath by enduring it for us on the cross.

## ▶ Whole-Bible Connections

**FEASTING IN GOD'S PRESENCE.** History begins and ends with a joyful feast in the presence of God. In Eden, God gave humanity "every tree that is pleasant to the sight and good for food" (Gen. 2:9, 16–17). Because Adam and Eve rejected this generosity, we are separated from God to eat in frustration (Gen.

39

3:19). Yet God is reopening the way to his festive table. He welcomed Israel's elders up Mount Sinai, where "they beheld God, and ate and drank" (Ex. 24:11). Through Isaiah, he tells us that people from all nations will come to his table: God will "make for all peoples a feast of rich food, a feast of well-aged wine" (Isa. 25:6). Picking up on this promise, Jesus compared his coming kingdom to a wedding feast (Matt. 22:2) and provided signposts to it with his abundant provisions of food and wine (Mark 6:30–44; 8:1–10; John 2:1–11). As the redeemed eat the Lord's Supper, we enjoy an appetizer to the coming banquet, purchased by his death (Luke 22:14, 16). When Jesus returns, he will restore and ratchet up the feast of Eden, spreading a banquet for all who trust in him. "Blessed are those who are invited to the marriage supper of the Lamb" (Rev. 19:9).

**DEATH DEFEATED.** Death, like sin and sickness and sorrow, does not belong in this world God created. Death is a curse, introduced in response to our rebellion against God (Gen. 2:17). Yet we read in Isaiah that God "will swallow up death forever" (Isa. 25:8). When? This triumph began when Jesus walked out of his own tomb two thousand years ago. He "abolished death and brought life and immortality to light through the gospel" (2 Tim. 1:10). But we still await the complete victory. He will return, raise his people from their graves, and overthrow death, which is "the last enemy to be destroyed" (1 Cor. 15:26). Paul celebrates this with an allusion to Isaiah's promise: "Then shall come to pass the saying that is written: 'Death is swallowed up in victory'" (1 Cor. 15:54; see Isa. 25:8).

## Theological Soundings

**RESURRECTION.** "Your dead shall live; their bodies shall rise. You who dwell in the dust, awake and sing for joy!" (Isa. 26:19). The Christian hope extends beyond death. When those who trust in Christ die, their bodies remain on earth and their spirits depart to be with Christ in heaven (Phil. 1:23). Even then, we still await the day when our bodies are raised from the dead and we will live physically and eternally with Christ on a new earth. The resurrection of Jesus is the pattern and hope of our future resurrection in his likeness (1 Cor. 15:20–23, 50–57).

**SPIRITUAL POWERS.** "On that day the LORD will punish the host of heaven, in heaven, and the kings of the earth, on the earth" (Isa. 24:21). Isaiah refers to the rebellion of human kings, but also that of spiritual beings in heaven. Such forces are aligned against the church even today: "For we do not wrestle against flesh and blood, but against the rulers, against the authorities, against the cosmic powers over this present darkness, against the spiritual forces of evil in the heavenly places" (Eph. 6:12). Yet Jesus has been exalted above them (Eph. 1:20–22) and God's wisdom in the gospel is being made known "to the rulers and authorities in the heavenly places" (3:10). God has already announced their final judgment through Isaiah.

## ▶ Personal Implications

Take time to reflect on the implications of Isaiah 24–27 for your own life today. Consider what you have learned that might lead you to praise God, repent of sin, and trust in his gracious promises. Make notes below on the personal implications for your walk with the Lord of (1) the *Gospel Glimpses*, (2) the *Whole-Bible Connections*, (3) the *Theological Soundings*, and (4) this passage as a whole.

### 1. Gospel Glimpses

### 2. Whole-Bible Connections

### 3. Theological Soundings

## 4. Isaiah 24–27

---

> ## As You Finish This Unit . . .

Take a moment now to ask for the Lord's blessing and help as you continue in this study of Isaiah. And take a moment also to look back through this unit of study, to reflect on some key things that the Lord may be teaching you—and perhaps to highlight and underline these things to review again in the future.

### Definitions

[1] **Apocalyptic** – A distinctive literary form of books such as Revelation and Daniel 7–12. These parts of Scripture include revelation about the future, highly symbolic imagery, and the underlying belief, dramatically presented, that God himself will one day change the present form of this world and establish his kingdom on earth.

[2] **Day of Atonement** – The holiest day in the Israelite calendar, when atonement was made for all the sins of Israel from the past year (Leviticus 16). Only on that day each year could someone—the high priest—enter the Most Holy Place of the tabernacle (later, the temple) and offer the necessary sacrifices. A "scapegoat" would also be sent into the wilderness as a sign of Israel's sins being carried away.

# Week 6: Sovereign Rebukes and Comforting Promises to the World

Isaiah 28:1–35:10

With a sixfold exclamation of dissatisfaction: "Ah!" (Isa. 28:1; 29:1, 15; 30:1; 33:1), Isaiah 28–33 proclaims God's rebuke to his people for choosing political expediency over trusting his promises. The warnings of judgment and promises of grace strung throughout these chapters come to a climax in Isaiah 34–35, where we hear of final judgment for the wicked and glorious hope for the trusting. In giving us this insight into history, God shows himself to be worthy of trust.

In Isaiah 28–35, God expresses great dissatisfaction in his faithless people, yet he remains steadfastly committed to fulfilling his gracious promises to them.

> ## Reflection and Discussion

Read through Isaiah 28–35, which will be the focus of this week's study. Following this, review the questions below and write your responses concerning this section of the book of Isaiah. (For further background, see the *ESV Study Bible*, pages 1288–1302; also available online at esv.org.)

### 1. Six Laments, with Promises (chs. 28–33)

The first proclamation of woe ("Ah!") is against God's people: The northern kingdom of Israel, here called "Ephraim" (Isa. 28:1–6), and the southern kingdom of Judah (28:7–13). Because the leaders scoff at Isaiah's message as beneath their intelligence (vv. 9–10; see 1 Cor. 2:14), God will now only speak to them by the foreign tongue of Assyrian invaders (vv. 11–13). How does this relate to Isaiah 6:9–12? How is this also a warning for today?

Review Isaiah 28:14–16 closely. Jerusalem's leaders rejoiced over their alliance with Egypt for protection from Assyria, "the overwhelming whip" (v. 15; see 30:1–5; 31:1–3). But Isaiah sees they are making "lies" their "refuge." What does he mean (note similar language in 30:2–3, 12; 31:1; Rom. 1:25)? How does this show us what is really going on when we look to something or someone other than God for ultimate security? Why would Isaiah call their agreement with Egypt a "covenant with death" (Isa. 28:15)?

How is God's response to Israel's sin in Isaiah 28:16 both a promise and a warning? Consider how this is ultimately fulfilled in the New Testament (1 Pet. 2:4–8; also Rom. 9:33; 10:11).

The people of Jerusalem (here called "Ariel") are rebuked for hypocritical worship. They "honor me with their lips," God says, "while their hearts are far from me" (Isa. 29:13; see Matt. 15:8–9). Outwardly proper worship offends God if it is a way of evading him at a deeper level. What does this tell us about worship and what God desires?

The stubbornness of Israel described in Isaiah 30:1–17 brings an unexpected response: "Therefore the LORD waits to be gracious to you" (v. 18). What does this tell us about God's character? Verses 19–26 show us how this grace will transform the world. What will it be like?

In a fifth woe, God calls his people to stop trusting in Egypt's help and turn back to him (Isa. 31:1–9), for he will defeat their enemies (32:8–9), enthrone his Messiah (vv. 1–8), and pour out his Spirit (vv. 15–18). What will be the results of the Messiah's rule and the outpouring of the Spirit? How does Acts 2 (note especially Acts 2:32–33) show that the fulfillment has begun?

God will destroy Assyria, the "destroyer" (Isa. 33:1). Isaiah describes God's overthrow of the Assyrian threat in his own time to portray the ultimate overthrow of wickedness in the future. What do we learn about God's character and promises in chapter 33?

## 2. Two Final Outcomes: Judgment and Salvation (chs. 34–35)

Isaiah describes God's final judgment for the world (Isaiah 34) and everlasting salvation for his people (ch. 35). Some interpreters have noted that judgment is described as an intensification of the curse[1] and a return to pre-creation chaos (Isaiah 34; see Gen. 1:2; 3:17–18), while salvation is described as a reversal of the curse and restoration of pre-fall flourishing (Isaiah 35; Genesis 1–2). What in these chapters leads to such conclusions?

Jesus alludes to Isaiah 35:5–6 in response to a question about his identity and mission. Read Matthew 11:2–6. What is Jesus' point? How does Isaiah 35:5–6 and the surrounding context help us understand what Jesus began to do at his first coming and will bring to completion at his second coming?

Read through the following three sections on *Gospel Glimpses*, *Whole-Bible Connections*, and *Theological Soundings*. Then take time to consider the *Personal Implications* these sections may have for you.

## Gospel Glimpses

**HOPE FOR THE ANXIOUS HEART.** In this fallen world, many are weighed down with various anxieties, fears, and troubles. Isaiah has a word for the worried: "Say to those who have an anxious heart, 'Be strong; fear not!'" (Isa. 35:4). Why? "Behold, your God will come with vengeance, with the recompense of God. He will come and save you" (v. 4). The way to fight anxiety is not to forget our problems or increase our self-confidence. Freedom from fear comes through hoping in God and his promises. The cross of Christ shows that God has, indeed, come to save us. No matter how uncertain our immediate future, we can trust that he is with us, he is for us, and he will never leave us or forsake us.

**A PATIENT GOD.** "Therefore the LORD waits to be gracious to you. . . . He will surely be gracious to you at the sound of your cry. As soon as he hears it, he answers you" (Isa. 30:18–19). God says this to people who want nothing to do with him. They are rebellious children who refuse to trust their Father (vv. 9–15). Judgment will come, to be sure (v. 17). Yet, even then, God stands ready to pour out fresh grace. This is the patience of God. And this is hope for sinners. Even as we continued to reject God, Christ died for us (Rom. 5:8). And he waits patiently for many to turn to him, for he is "not wishing that any should perish, but that all should reach repentance" (2 Pet. 3:9).

## Whole-Bible Connections

**HEALING.** Isaiah promises that one day the blind will see, the deaf will hear, the lame will leap, and the mute will sing (Isa. 29:18–19; 35:5–6). Disabilities such as these did not always exist. They entered the world because of humanity's sin and remain as a sober reminder of our spiritual brokenness. But, as we hear in Isaiah, God will bring both spiritual and physical restoration to all who trust him. When Jesus came, he began to roll back the curse, giving sight to the blind, hearing to the deaf, strength to the lame, and voice to the mute (Matt. 11:4–5). This was a foretaste of what he will do for all his people when he returns. But it will happen only because, even as he healed others, Jesus was on his way to the grave where he would lie dead—literally blind, deaf, lame, and mute—for three days. He took our sin and brokenness so that we might receive forgiveness and healing.

**REVERSAL OF THE CURSE.** "Thorns shall grow over its strongholds, nettles and thistles in its fortresses" (Isa. 34:13). This is not the first time judgment is described in terms of thorns and thistles in Isaiah (5:6; 7:23, 25; 32:13). Nor is it the first time in the Bible, for the ground was covered with them after humanity's first sin (Gen. 3:17–18). Thorns are a sign of the curse. But Isaiah points forward to its reversal as he exults in the future flourishing of the ground, when "the wilderness and the dry land shall be glad; . . . it shall blossom abundantly" (Isa. 35:1–2; see also 27:4; 32:13–15; 55:13). The curse over all of creation, and the curse over all of us, can be lifted only because Jesus became a curse for us (Gal. 3:13). In a suggestively symbolic action, thorns were lifted from the ground and placed upon Jesus' own head at the cross (Matt. 27:29). Since this returned true "joy to the world," we can sing, "No more let sins and sorrows grow, nor thorns infest the ground. He comes to make his blessings flow far as the curse is found."

## Theological Soundings

**THE WRATH OF GOD.** God sometimes uses nations to carry out his judgment. Standing behind the nations is the Lord himself, a divine warrior who encamps against his people and besieges them with towers (Isa. 29:3; see 42:13). With battle shouts and songs, "he will fight with [Assyria]" (30:32). With a settled opposition to evil, God fights against the wicked. Indeed, John's vision shows Jesus coming with the armies of heaven as a warrior, carrying out God's judgment (Rev. 19:11–21).

**GOD'S SOVEREIGNTY IN SALVATION.** God will renew the creation (Isa. 29:17–21) and restore his people (vv. 22–24). "Those who go astray in spirit will come to understanding" (v. 24). This is all God's sovereign[2] work, which is why he calls his revived people "the work of my hands" (v. 23; also 19:25; 60:21). Ultimately, God must receive all credit for the salvation of sinners. If we can look back over our lives and see repentance and faith, we are witnessing the work of God's hands. Revival, renewal, and salvation belong to God.

**DEITY OF JESUS.** The expectation of a coming king from the line of David continues in Isaiah 32:1: "Behold, a king will reign in righteousness" (see Isa. 9:6–7; 11:1–5). But, surprisingly, this coming king is also called Yahweh, the LORD: "The LORD is our king; he will save us" (33:22). This, of course, creates a tension. Will this coming king be a man from the line of David or will it be God himself? The answer is, both. Jesus, God in the flesh, is fully divine and fully human.

## Personal Implications

Take time to reflect on the implications of Isaiah 28–35 for your own life today. Consider what you have learned that might lead you to praise God, repent of sin, and trust in his gracious promises. Make notes below on the personal implications for your walk with the Lord of (1) the *Gospel Glimpses*, (2) the *Whole-Bible Connections*, (3) the *Theological Soundings*, and (4) this passage as a whole.

## 1. Gospel Glimpses

## 2. Whole-Bible Connections

## 3. Theological Soundings

## 4. Isaiah 28–35

-------------------------------------------------------------

-------------------------------------------------------------

-------------------------------------------------------------

-------------------------------------------------------------

-------------------------------------------------------------

-------------------------------------------------------------

> ## As You Finish This Unit . . .

Take a moment now to ask for the Lord's blessing and help as you continue in this study of Isaiah. And take a moment also to look back through this unit of study, to reflect on some key things that the Lord may be teaching you—and perhaps to highlight and underline these things to review again in the future.

### Definitions

[1] **The curse** – In response to Adam and Eve's rebellion against him, God cursed Satan, humanity, and the entire creation (Gen. 3:14–19). Yet God also promised to bring blessing back to the world, thus reversing the curse and restoring the original blessing of creation (Gen. 3:15; 12:1–3). The ultimate fulfillment of these promises is still to come.

[2] **Sovereignty** – Supreme and independent power and authority. Sovereignty over all things is a distinctive attribute of God (1 Tim. 6:15–16). He directs all things to carry out his purposes (Rom. 8:28–29).

# WEEK 7:
# THE DELIVERING
# GRACE OF GOD

Isaiah 36:1–39:8

## The Place of the Passage

Surrounded by poetry on either side, Isaiah 36–39 is a narrative bridge that links chapters 1–35 with 40–66. Isaiah previously proclaimed that God would judge Israel's enemies and save those who trust him. Can God be trusted to do this? In chapters 36–39, God acts concretely in history to rescue his people from attack, answering this question in the affirmative. This section also provides the context for chapters 40–55, as Isaiah tells Hezekiah that the nation is doomed to exile in Babylon.

## The Big Picture

Isaiah 36–39 demonstrates that God can be trusted to fulfill his promises and that Israel will be sent in to exile in Babylon.

## Reflection and Discussion

Read through the complete passage for this study, Isaiah 36–39. Then review the questions below and write your notes on them concerning this transitional section in the book of Isaiah. (For further background, see the *ESV Study Bible*, pages 1302–1309; also available online at esv.org.)

### 1. God's Delivering Grace for Judah (chs. 36–37)

In 701 BC Sennacherib, the king of Assyria, sent an army with the Rabshakeh, an Assyrian military officer, to Jerusalem to pressure King Hezekiah to surrender. Note the familiar location mentioned in Isaiah 36:2 (see 7:3). In what ways is the situation described in 36:1–9 similar to that of 7:1–9, which involved Hezekiah's father, Ahaz?

The Rabshakeh asks Hezekiah, "In whom do you now trust?" (Isa. 36:5). In that pointed question he unknowingly poses one of Isaiah's central questions for his readers. The word "trust" appears seven times in the Hebrew text of this paragraph (36:4–7, 9). What lies and half-truths does the Rabshakeh tell Hezekiah and Israel in an attempt to weaken their faith[1] (36:5–20)?

Hezekiah dramatically repents and seeks a word from God through Isaiah (Isa. 37:1–2). How is this response different than that of his father, Ahaz, described in chapter 7? In light of this, as well as his prayer in 37:15–20, in what ways is Hezekiah a model for Israel in the midst of crisis?

It may seem that Sennacherib and the Rabshakeh are merely taunting Judah and King Hezekiah. But God is the one who is mocked. How does Isaiah 37 show us, at each step of the way, that God's glory is the central issue (note Isa. 37:4, 6, 10, 16–20, 23–24, 35)?

Isaiah 37:35 gives the twofold reason for God's deliverance of Jerusalem. At first, the statement about David may seem out of place. But read 2 Sam. 7:12–13; Isa. 9:7; 11:1, Rom. 1:1–5, and Rev. 22:16. How do these texts help us understand the statement's significance?

## 2. God's Delivering Grace for Hezekiah (chs. 38–39)

How are the events described in Isaiah 38:1–6 similar to those of the previous two chapters? Additionally, what does God's response to Hezekiah teach us about God and about prayer?

We have now seen God respond to prayer by acting in history to save his people (Isa. 37:36–38) and to extend their king's life (38:4–8). How does this relate to chapters 1–35, which contains God's promises to judge and redeem? How would this strengthen their hope?

Through Isaiah, God tells Hezekiah of his people's future exile, when everything "shall be carried to Babylon" (Isa. 39:6). Like Hezekiah's recovery from sickness, Israel's deliverance from Assyria will be temporary. This prepares the way for the assumed setting of Isaiah 40–55, which envisions God's people in captivity in Babylon. Read 2 Kings 24:10–25:21. What were the key events in the exile of Judah? Why, according to 2 Kings 23:26–27, was Judah sent away?

How does Isaiah 39 show Hezekiah's wavering faith? This failure leaves us convinced that he is not the promised righteous king (Isa. 9:6–7; 11:1–5). How does this create a sense of longing as we head into the rest of the book?

Read through the following three sections on *Gospel Glimpses, Whole-Bible Connections*, and *Theological Soundings*. Then take time to consider the *Personal Implications* these sections may have for you.

## Gospel Glimpses

**WHY GOD SAVES.** Hezekiah asks God to deliver Israel for God's sake, not their own: "Save us from his hand, that all the kingdoms of the earth may know that you alone are the LORD" (Isa. 37:20). God responds by saving them for his glory and for the advancement of his saving purposes in the world (37:35; also 43:25; 48:9–11). There is no firmer foundation for our salvation than this. Our merits are out of the question—what a relief! When we're at our worst, we can still appeal to God for grace, not because we deserve it, but because it shows him to be the God that he is: A merciful God who delights to shower his blessings on undeserving sinners who simply come to him with open hands.

**ANSWERED PRAYER.** There are two crises here, both of which end in deliverance through prayer. Jerusalem's existence is threatened, Hezekiah prays, and God saves (Isaiah 36–37). Hezekiah's life is threatened, he prays, and God saves (ch. 38). In both cases, God delivered in direct response to humble, desperate prayer (37:21ff; 38:5–6). God does not stand aloof when his people look to him as their only hope. Because Jesus is our sinless high priest, we can draw near to God's throne of grace with confidence, "that we may receive mercy and find grace to help in time of need" (Heb. 4:15–16).

## Whole-Bible Connections

**AN INTERCEDING KING.** In response to Hezekiah's prayer, God promised not only to extend his life but also to deliver Jerusalem from attack (Isa. 38:5–6). What was Hezekiah's prayer? "Please, O LORD, remember how I have walked before you in faithfulness and with a whole heart, and have done what is good in your sight" (v. 3). Judah was too sinful to appeal to their own righteousness. But Hezekiah, a faithful king in the line of David, interceded[2] for them and was heard (2 Kings 19:14–19). This shows our need for a righteous king to step in and pray for us. Yet even Hezekiah is no ideal figure, for he still wavers in faith (Isa. 39:1–8). This points us forward to the Davidic king more righteous than Hezekiah: Jesus Christ, who is risen from the dead and "always lives to make intercession for [us]" (Heb. 7:25; also Rom. 8:34).

**EXILE.** God created Adam and Eve, placed them in the garden in Eden, and called them to trust him. When they rebelled, God exiled them from the garden and his presence (Gen. 3:23). The story is repeated with Israel. God created them, placed them in the land of Canaan, and called them to trust him. If they did, they would dwell with God (Lev. 26:3–13). If they rebelled, they would be exiled from the land and his presence (Lev. 26:33; Deut. 28:36–41). Mirroring the story of Eden, they rebelled and were exiled to Babylon, which Isaiah foretold to Hezekiah (Isa. 39:6–7; see Jer. 52:3). The prophets promise a day when all of God's people, Israel as well as the nations, will return to his presence. This will happen because of Jesus Christ, who succeeded where Adam, Israel, and all humanity failed. Although he is the only one who deserves to remain with his Father, he was cast away and cried out, "My God, my God, why have you forsaken me?" (Matt. 27:46). He took the ultimate exile of hell so that we don't have to. He was exiled so that we could return. As we are restored to his presence through faith, we now await the day when we'll live with him forever in a new and better Eden (Rev. 21:1–22:5).

## Theological Soundings

**GOD'S TRUSTWORTHINESS.** Leading up to Isaiah 36–37, Isaiah has repeatedly called God's people to trust God's promises. But how do we know he can be trusted? The Assyrian leaders say, "Do not let your God in whom you trust deceive you by promising that Jerusalem will not be given into the hand of the king of Assyria" (37:10). But God shows up and acts concretely within history, striking the Assyrians and rescuing Jerusalem (37:36–38). God's actions in the past prove his faithfulness, securing his promises for the future, that we might trust him in the present. The supreme reason we can trust God is his sending of his Son on our behalf—"He who did not spare his own Son but gave him up for us all, how will he not also with him graciously give us all things?" (Rom. 8:32).

**FAITH.** "On what do you rest this trust of yours?" (Isa. 36:4). This question, which the Assyrian leader asked Hezekiah, is the fundamental question Isaiah asks all of us. From beginning to end, the Bible calls people to wholehearted reliance on God. In this context, we see that faith is resting in and leaning on someone for deliverance and security (36:4–6, 15). The Bible calls us away from reliance on ourselves or anyone else to save us. Only God, through Jesus Christ, is able to give us ultimate deliverance and security.

## Personal Implications

Take time to reflect on the implications of Isaiah 36–39 for your own life today. Consider what you have learned that might lead you to praise God, repent of sin, and trust in his gracious promises. Make notes below on the personal implications for your walk with the Lord of (1) the *Gospel Glimpses*, (2) the *Whole-Bible Connections*, (3) the *Theological Soundings*, and (4) this passage as a whole.

### 1. Gospel Glimpses

### 2. Whole-Bible Connections

57

## 3. Theological Soundings

## 4. Isaiah 36–39

## As You Finish This Unit . . .

Take a moment now to ask for the Lord's blessing and help as you continue in this study of Isaiah. And take a moment also to look back through this unit of study, to reflect on some key things that the Lord may be teaching you—and perhaps to highlight and underline these things to review again in the future.

### Definitions

[1] **Faith** – Trust in or reliance upon something or someone. Salvation, which is purely a work of God's grace, can be received only through faith (Rom. 5:2; Eph. 2:8–9).

[2] **Intercession** – Appealing to one person on behalf of another. Often used with reference to prayer.

# WEEK 8:
# COMFORT FOR ISRAEL
# AND THE WORLD

Isaiah 40:1 48:22

## The Place of the Passage

In the first 39 chapters, Isaiah addressed his 8th-century BC contemporaries. This section climaxed with the prediction of an exile to Babylon (39:6–7), which would end up occurring in the 6th century BC (586) when the Babylonians destroyed Jerusalem and took Israel captive. In chapters 40–55, Isaiah addresses those of this future exiled generation with words of hope. Through Isaiah, God comforts his people with the good news of his return as king to bring physical and spiritual redemption.

## The Big Picture

In Isaiah 40–48, God proclaims the comforting message of his redemption of his people from their physical exile and spiritual bondage.

> ### Reflection and Discussion

**Read the entire text for this week's study, Isaiah 40–48. Then review the following questions and write your notes on them concerning this section of Isaiah. (For further background, see the _ESV Study Bible_, pages 1309–1330; also available online at esv.org.)**

### 1. Comfort for Israel and the World (40:1–42:17)

Through Isaiah, God proclaims a message of comfort to the brokenhearted, exiled generation. This message is "good news" (Isa. 40:9). What are the key elements of this announcement in 40:1–11?

A forerunner will announce the return of God to his people, when he will reveal his glory, establish his kingdom, and shepherd his people (Isa. 40:3–5, 10–11). John the Baptist found in these words his own calling to his generation, implying that the promises of these chapters had not yet fully come to pass (v. 3; Mark 1:1–8). Whose presence did John end up introducing? What are the implications for how we understand who Jesus is (his identity) and what he came to do (his mission)?

At the heart of the good news is the presence of God: "Behold your God!" (Isa. 40:9). Thus, it is not surprising that we find his glorious character displayed in the ensuing verses. What, specifically, do these verses proclaim about God's incomparable greatness (v. 12), wisdom (vv. 13–14), immensity (vv. 15–17), sovereignty (vv. 22–23), and strength (vv. 25–28)?

A central phrase in Isaiah 41:8–20 is, "Fear not" (41:10, 14; also 43:1, 5; 44:2, 8). Why would the people have been afraid? What reasons does God give to dispel their fear (vv. 8–14)? What is the effect of the repetition of "I"?

The first of four Servant Songs is Isaiah 42:1–9 (also 49:1–13; 50:4–9; 52:13–53:12). Isaiah sprinkles references to his "servant" in chapters 41–48, often as a title for his people as a whole (e.g., 41:8–9; 42:19; 43:10; 44:1–2). Here in 42:1–9, the servant is best explained as a true and faithful Israel. It is the nation as it should be, faithful to their calling and mission. What is this servant called to do?

## 2. National and Spiritual Redemption for God's people (42:18–44:23)

As the Israelites read of the servant in Isaiah 42:1–9, they would have seen a description of their own calling. But how do verses 18–25 show us that Israel, although identified as God's "servant" (v. 19), has failed? How do we see that they need deliverance just as much as the nations (compare 42:18, 22 with 42:7)? Yet how does God view them and what will he do for them (43:1–7)?

How does Isaiah show the folly of idolatry[1] in Isaiah 44:9–20? The sketch of idol worship is bracketed with a description of the true God (44:6–8, 21–22). How is God different, and why, therefore, is it the height of wisdom to turn to him? As you reflect on this, consider similar contrasts in 40:18–20; 41:21–24; 46:5–7.

## 3. God's Surprising Method of National Deliverance (44:24–48:22)

In Isaiah 44:24–45:8, we hear of God's plan to use Cyrus the Great, leader of the rising Persian empire, to conquer Babylon and release Israel to return to their land. How does Israel respond to this plan (45:9–10)? Summarize the Lord's reply (vv. 11–13).

God's plan goes beyond the return of his people to Jerusalem. His salvation has a worldwide reach (Isa. 45:14–25). What does Paul's use of Isaiah 45:23 in Philippians 2:9–11 tell us about the One to whom the world must submit?

Isaiah 46–47 draws our attention to the downfall of Babylon, together with their pride and false gods. Yet how is Israel just as sinful (Isa. 48:1–8)? What, then, is the deepest motive in the heart of God for rescuing his people (vv. 9–11)?

Read through the following three sections on *Gospel Glimpses*, *Whole-Bible Connections*, and *Theological Soundings*. Then take time to consider the *Personal Implications* these sections may have for you.

## Gospel Glimpses

**FEAR NOT.** Israel has reason to fear. They have rejected God and have been taken captive by a ruthless nation. Yet God does not say, "Fear, for I have forsaken you; be dismayed, for I am no longer your God; I will not help you." Just the opposite: "Fear not, for I am with you; be not dismayed, for I am your God; ... I will help you" (Isa. 41:10). When grace is backed by infinite power, it casts out fear. The God who offers to help us is the one who measured the waters in his hand, stretched out the heavens like a curtain, and calls the stars by name (40:12, 22, 26).

**HONORED SINNERS.** Because of Israel's continual sin against God, they deserve judgment. "Was it not the LORD," they said, "against whom we have sinned?" (Isa. 42:24). But God's response is counterintuitive: "But now thus says the LORD . . . Fear not, for I have redeemed you; I have called you by name, you are mine" (43:1). Most astonishing of all, perhaps, is how God views his sinful people. He says, "you are precious in my eyes, and honored, and I love you" (v. 4). Precious, honored, and loved! We would expect God to speak such words only to his own Son. But, in grace, he says it to all who trust him. United to Christ, we too become God's own children, precious and loved.

## Whole-Bible Connections

**NEW EXODUS.** At the exodus, God displayed his glory in cloud and fire, made a way through the sea, and led his people out of Egyptian bondage to the Promised Land. Israel is enslaved again, this time in Babylon. Isaiah prophesies a recapitulation[2] of the exodus story in the future. God will lead his people in a New Exodus redemption, where they will be set free from their bondage not just to Babylon, but to sin. God will display his glory and make a "way" for his people, this time through the wilderness, leading them back to Jerusalem (40:3–5; also 11:11–16; 43:16–21; 51:10–11; 52:12; Jer. 16:14–15). Although a few returned home in the sixth century BC, the ultimate New Exodus would occur through the ministry, death, and resurrection of Jesus (Mark 1:1–3; see also Luke 9:31). Jesus set his people free from their slavery to sin and death and opened the way back to God's presence.

**THE SERVANT.** In Genesis 12:1–3, God promised Abraham he would become a great nation and that, through him, "all the families of the earth shall be blessed." From the beginning, this great nation of Israel was to be God's servant, advancing his purposes in the world. Their obedience to God's law would reflect his character to the world, attracting the nations with a moral magnetism (Isa. 42:21; see Deut. 4:5–8). Although they were to be "a light for the nations, to open the eyes that are blind" (Isa. 42:6–7), they were themselves spiritually blind (vv. 18–19). Israel and the nations remained in darkness until Jesus, the true and better servant, took up Israel's mission as the light of the world, giving sight to the blind, both physically and spiritually (John 8:12; 9:5–7).

## Theological Soundings

**SIN AS IDOLATRY.** Isaiah gives extensive space to describing the process of idolatry, from the beginning stages of crafting an idol to the culmination of worship (Isa. 44:9–20). Even the tediousness and length of Isaiah's description causes us to feel something of the burden of idolatry. Yet all the labor of serving an idol does not result in any kind of salvation. Idolatry is looking to anything or anyone other than God to be our refuge and source of joy. But it is a false hope, for idols do not deliver (44:17, 20; 46:7; 57:13). Sin isn't just doing the wrong things; it is, more fundamentally, looking to the wrong places for salvation, joy, security, and peace. It is idolatry.

**GOD'S FOREKNOWLEDGE.** Through Isaiah, God displays his glory by proclaiming his foreknowledge. He is the first and the last, "declaring the end from the beginning" (Isa. 44:6–8; 46:10). God intentionally established a pattern of prophecies and then faithfully fulfilled them. Why? To uphold his honor and secure his people's trust. "I declared them to you from of old, before they came to pass I announced them to you," he declares, "lest you should say, 'My idol did them'" (48:5). Idols are worthless. They do not know the past and cannot tell the future (41:21–24). The foreknowledge of God, clearly set forth in Isaiah, displays God as worthy of wholehearted trust.

> ## Personal Implications

Take time to reflect on the implications of Isaiah 40–48 for your own life today. Consider what you have learned that might lead you to praise God, repent of sin, and trust in his gracious promises. Make notes below on the personal implications for your walk with the Lord of (1) the *Gospel Glimpses*, (2) the *Whole-Bible Connections*, (3) the *Theological Soundings*, and (4) this passage as a whole.

## 1. Gospel Glimpses

## 2. Whole-Bible Connections

## 3. Theological Soundings

## 4. Isaiah 40–48

## As You Finish This Unit . . .

Take a moment now to ask for the Lord's blessing and help as you continue in this study of Isaiah. And take a moment also to look back through this unit of study, to reflect on some key things that the Lord may be teaching you—and perhaps to highlight and underline these things to review again in the future.

### Definitions

[1] **Idolatry** – In the Bible, often refers to the worship of a physical object. Paul's comments in Colossians 3:5 suggest that idolatry can include covetousness, since it is essentially equivalent to worshiping material things. It is looking to anything, good or bad, to provide what only God can give.

[2] **Recapitulation** – The repeating of an earlier event or story. This later repetition generally involves a heightening of significance.

# WEEK 9: THE SUFFERING AND TRIUMPHANT SERVANT

Isaiah 49:1–55:13

## The Place of the Passage

Isaiah 40–48 introduced the message of Israel's coming restoration. Through Cyrus, God will bring his people home from exile and return them to their land. In addition to national restoration, God's people are also in need of spiritual salvation. Their deeper problem of sin and idolatry requires a deeper solution. According to Isaiah 49–55 this will be accomplished through the work of a "servant," who will die for the sins of God's people and emerge in victory, bringing about forgiveness and restoration.

## The Big Picture

Isaiah 49–55 tells us that God's unrighteous people will be saved through the work of a righteous, suffering servant.

## Reflection and Discussion

Read through the complete text for this study, Isaiah 49–55. Then review the questions below and write your notes on them concerning this central text of Isaiah. (For further background, see the *ESV Study Bible*, pages 1330–1342; also available online at esv.org.)

### 1. The Servant Displayed, God's People Assured (49:1–52:12)

Immediately after Isaiah introduced the ideal servant (Isa. 42:1–7), we learned that the people of Israel failed to be the servant of God and light to the nations that they were called to be (42:18–25). Now 49:1–13 introduces us to an individual servant, called "Israel" in verse 3. How does verse 5 show us that this servant, although embodying the nation of Israel (v. 3), is nevertheless distinct from them? In what ways do we see that his mission is to fulfill that of 42:1–7 (compare 49:5–6, 8–9 with 42:6–7)? How is his mission more expansive in light of Israel's failure to be the true servant (consider 49:5 in light of 42:18–25)?

What repetition do we see in Isaiah 49:23, 26? Note similar statements in 45:3, 6; and 60:16. This "recognition formula" derives from God's actions at the exodus (read Ex. 6:7 and 14:18 within their contexts). What does this teach us about God's ultimate purposes in judging and saving?

In the third of four servant passages, we see the servant sustaining others through his teaching (Isa. 50:4–9). What, specifically, do we learn about him?

Israel longs for God to "awake" from his supposed slumber and redeem them (Isa. 51:9–11). God turns their cry back on them, calling them to "awaken" because redemption draws near (51:12–52:12). What are the central elements of this glad proclamation of salvation in 52:7–11? What key terms or ideas from 40:1–11 are emphasized or expanded here? How does 2 Samuel 18:19, 24–27 help us understand the imagery of Isaiah 52:7–8?

## 2. The Sin-Bearing Work of the Servant (52:13–53:12)

The fourth and final servant text is a carefully developed poem of five stanzas of three verses each (Isa. 52:13–53:12). What do quotations of these verses in the New Testament—such as Mark 10:45; Acts 8:30–35; and 1 Peter 2:22–25—suggest to us about the ultimate fulfillment of this passage?

The central stanza is the heart of the passage (Isa. 53:4–6). What did the servant do? For what purpose? How does this resolve the tension that has been developing throughout the book: If God is truly the "Holy One of Israel," and his people are utterly sinful and deserving of judgment, how can God pour out his blessing on them?

What do we learn from the second and fourth stanzas (Isa. 53:1–3, 7–9) about how the servant would be viewed and treated by those to whom he was sent? How do various aspects of this description come to fruition in Jesus' life, ministry, death, and burial?

What does Isaiah 53:10–12 tell us about the divine purpose behind the human oppression of the servant? How is this perspective present in Acts 2:22–23 and 4:27–28? Additionally, how does Isaiah 53:10–12 demonstrate that the servant arose victoriously after his suffering?

## 3. The Results of the Servant's Work (54:1–55:13)

By suffering the ultimate exile for his people, the servant accomplishes the promised restoration. How does Isaiah use the metaphors of Israel as a barren woman (Isa. 54:1–3) and widow (vv. 4–8) to creatively express the glorious salvation provided by the servant's work? What is the main point?

According to Isaiah 55:1, who is invited to enjoy God's salvation? What is required of all who will receive God's free gift of salvation (vv. 2–3, 6–9)?

Read through the following three sections on *Gospel Glimpses*, *Whole-Bible Connections*, and *Theological Soundings*. Then take time to consider the *Personal Implications* these sections may have for you.

> ## Gospel Glimpses

**DIVINE COMPASSION.** The proclamation "comfort my people" from Isaiah 40:1 echoes throughout the rest of the book. Isaiah 49:13, for instance, calls upon the whole cosmos to "Sing for joy! . . . For the LORD has comforted his people" (similarly, 49:15; 54:7–8, 10; 55:7). Isaiah continually reassures us of God's great love for great sinners. Jesus tells of the Father's kindness toward all who have made a wreck of their lives like a prodigal son. When the son came home, "his father saw him and felt compassion, and ran and embraced him and kissed him" (Luke 15:20). Or, as Isaiah says, "let him return to the LORD, that he may have compassion on him . . . for he will abundantly pardon" (55:7).

**ABUNDANT SATISFACTION.** As a result of the servant's sacrifice, Isaiah issues a fourfold call to "*Come,* everyone who thirsts, *come* to the water . . . *come . . . come* . . . (Isa. 55:1). We learn four things about this invitation. First, God offers true satisfaction. We labor for that which doesn't satisfy, but God offers us a delightful feast (v. 2). Second, we find this satisfaction in God himself. Hence, the call to "seek *the* LORD" (v. 6). This joy, thirdly, is available to all: *everyone* who thirsts. Finally, it is scandalously free. Since the servant has already paid the price in his suffering (53:4–6), the only requirement is to come.

## Whole-Bible Connections

**THE TRUE PRIEST AND SACRIFICE.** The suffering servant, whose work brings about forgiveness and restoration (Isa. 52:13–53:12), is described as a priest. Just as Israelite priests cleansed people by sprinkling with blood, this servant will "sprinkle many nations" (Isa. 52:15; see Ex. 29:21; Lev. 16:14–19). Yet this priest is also the sacrifice. He is made "an offering for guilt," presenting himself as a sacrifice for a guilt offering (Isa. 53:10; see Lev. 5:15–17). According to Hebrews, this points forward to the work of Jesus, who is the true priest (Heb. 2:17; 4:14) and ultimate sacrifice (9:26), and whose sprinkled blood cleanses us from all our sin (9:13–14; 12:24).

**THE KINGDOM OF GOD.** "How beautiful upon the mountains are the feet of him who brings good news" (Isa. 52:7). It was not uncommon for a lone runner to sprint home to announce the fate of an Israelite battle. In this case, the runner returns to broadcast the "good news" of a victory, which results in "peace," "happiness," and "salvation" (v. 7). This imagery shows that a spiritual victory has been won ("Your God reigns"; vv. 7, 10). In light of the overarching story of redemption, this announces the dawn of the kingdom of God. Ever since the fall[1] of humanity, we have been in spiritual bondage and have not acknowledged God's kingship. Yet Isaiah announces the good news (v. 7, literally "gospel"), when God would come to overthrow evil, restore his people, and reign as king. This good news promised by Isaiah is fulfilled in Jesus, who said, "The time is fulfilled, and the kingdom of God is at hand; repent and believe in the gospel" (Mark 1:15). Through Jesus' life, death, and resurrection, the kingdom of God is being reestablished.

## Theological Soundings

**ATONEMENT.** "He was pierced for our transgressions" (Isa. 53:5). The servant of Isaiah 53 suffered and died because of sin. But it wasn't his own sin, for "there was no deceit in his mouth" (v. 9). It was for the sins of others. This is what theologians have called *penal substitutionary atonement*. He stood in the place of sinners as a *substitute*, bearing the *penalty* of their sins in his death, so that they might be forgiven and reconciled[2] to God. This atonement was ultimately accomplished through Jesus Christ on the cross, where, as 2 Corinthians 5:21 says, "For our sake he made him to be sin who knew no sin, so that in him we might become the righteousness of God."

**THE WORD OF GOD.** In Isaiah 55:10–11, God compares his word to rain, which produces new life and sustenance. God's words of promise are just as powerful and life-giving: "So shall my word be that goes out from my mouth," God says, "It shall not return to me empty, but it shall accomplish that which I purpose" (v. 11). Similarly, Hebrews says, "the word of God is living and active" (4:12). As we read the pages of the Bible and hear God's word preached, the Holy Spirit is using it to change us, giving and sustaining our lives like rain sustains the land.

## Personal Implications

Take time to reflect on the implications of Isaiah 49–55 for your own life today. Consider what you have learned that might lead you to praise God, repent of sin, and trust in his gracious promises. Make notes below on the personal implications for your walk with the Lord of (1) the *Gospel Glimpses*, (2) the *Whole-Bible Connections*, (3) the *Theological Soundings*, and (4) this passage as a whole.

### 1. Gospel Glimpses

### 2. Whole-Bible Connections

## 3. Theological Soundings

## 4. Isaiah 49–55

> ## As You Finish This Unit . . .

Take a moment now to ask for the Lord's blessing and help as you continue in this study of Isaiah. And take a moment also to look back through this unit of study, to reflect on some key things that the Lord may be teaching you—and perhaps to highlight and underline these things to review again in the future.

### Definitions

[1] **The fall** – Adam and Eve's disobedience of God by eating the fruit from the tree of the knowledge of good and evil, resulting in their loss of innocence and favor with God and the introduction of sin and its effects into the world (Genesis 3; Rom. 5:12–21; 1 Cor. 15:21–22).

[2] **Reconciliation** – The restoration of relationship and peace between alienated or opposing parties. Through his death and resurrection, Jesus has reconciled believers to God (2 Cor. 5:18–21).

# WEEK 10:
## SALVATION FOR THE
## NATIONS, JUDGMENT
## FOR THE WICKED

Isaiah 56:1–59:21

## The Place of the Passage

After addressing his contemporaries with the threat of judgment in Isaiah 1–39, Isaiah addressed the future exiled generation in chapters 40–55. He comforted them with the promise of restoration, which the servant of the Lord, the true Israel, would bring about through his sacrificial suffering and subsequent exaltation (52:13–53:12). Now in Isaiah 56–59, Isaiah begins to speak of the time when some of the exiles return home—as well as subsequent generations. Here we see that God opposes religious hypocrisy and redefines his people, welcoming the humble from any nation.

## The Big Picture

In Isaiah 56–59, God opposes the hypocritical and welcomes the humble from any nation.

> ## Reflection and Discussion

Read through the complete passage for this study, Isaiah 56–59. Then review the questions below and record your notes and reflections on this section of Isaiah's prophecy. (For further background, see the *ESV Study Bible*, pages 1342–1349; also available online at esv.org.)

Although Isaiah 40–55 emphasized the promise of salvation for exiled Israel, we have already seen that the servant's saving work issues forth a call to "*everyone* who thirsts" (55:1). Now in 56:1–8, salvation is explicitly shown to extend to the nations. What does God promise to give the foreigners who trust in him (vv. 6–8)? How does verse 8 expand the vision of 11:11–12? Does this shed light on what Jesus says in John 10:16?

How are the people of 57:1–13 characterized? It will help to note that the oaks, trees, rocks, and mountains are idolatrous places of worship. How does this contrast with the attitude present in verse 15? Looking back to 53:5, how is the "peace"[1] and "healing" found in 57:19 ultimately brought about?

What, according to Isaiah 58:1–5, did Israel do to show their religious zeal? What does Isaiah say that calls their sincerity into question?

What does true godliness look like, according to Isaiah 58:6–14? What might this look like today? How does this provide a similar picture to what we read in James 1:27?

How does Isaiah 59:2 help us understand the consequences of our sin? What ideas in verses 3–8 does Paul use in his description of humanity's sinfulness in Romans 3:9–18? What might a similar list look like if it described the common sins of our time?

The writing changes from second person ("you") in Isaiah 59:1–8 to first person ("we," "our") in vv. 9–13. What is the significance of this shift? How is their attitude similar to that of David in Psalm 51:3?

The sinfulness of Israel leaves them in a helpless situation. God observes that there is no one to intercede, no one to help (Isa. 59:15–16a). Though offended and "displeased" by their sin, what is God's response to their help-lessness (v.16b)? To gain a clearer understanding of what this means, consider how Isaiah uses the metaphor of God's "arm" in 51:9; 52:10; 53:1. How does this display of God's character give hope to any who have continually offended him?

God dresses himself as a warrior in Isaiah 59:17–19. What is he preparing to do? What will be the ultimate result?

There is a shift in Isaiah 59:21 from plural ("my covenant with them") to sin-gular ("my Spirit that is upon you"). How does v. 20 identify the individual that God begins speaking to in v. 21? With chapters 49–55 in mind, who do you say is this redeemer?

Read through the following three sections on *Gospel Glimpses*, *Whole-Bible Connections*, and *Theological Soundings*. Then take time to consider the *Personal Implications* these sections may have for you.

## Gospel Glimpses

**REVIVAL FOR THE HUMBLE.** "I dwell in the high and holy place, and also with him who is of a contrite and lowly spirit" (Isa. 57:15; similarly, 66:2). The God of the Bible is exalted in his holiness, too pure to look at evil (Hab. 1:13). Sinners who know this about him fear for their lives in his presence (Gen. 32:30; Ex. 33:20; Isa. 33:14; Luke 1:12). Yet he condescends to dwell "with him who is of a contrite and lowly spirit" (Isa. 57:15). Rather than destroying such people, he comes to revive[2] them (v. 15). God loves to breathe new life into his people. We have only to stay low before him.

**FULL ASSURANCE.** The foreigner of Isaiah 56:3 is timid. He knows that God is gracious, so he comes to him in faith. But there remains a lingering suspicion that "the LORD will surely separate me from his people." He is wrong, of course, as the wonderful promises of vv. 4–8 make clear. Like this foreigner, we often fail to comprehend the wonder of God's absolute, open-armed welcome in Christ. We may mentally grasp that every ounce of his wrath was poured out on his Son at the cross. Yet our timidity to approach him, especially when we contemplate our sinful failures, shows that we wonder if he might rather have us keep our distance. Though counterintuitive, the cross really does mean that, even though we deserve nothing but rejection, we may come to God with confidence and full assurance of faith (Heb. 10:19, 22). He welcomes us with open arms when we come to him for mercy.

## Whole-Bible Connections

**GLOBAL SALVATION.** As a result of the suffering servant's peace-making work (Isa. 52:13–53:12), the way is cleared for salvation to spread through Israel to the world. Any foreigner or eunuch who comes to God will be met with gracious acceptance (56:3–8; see also 57:19). The promise of worldwide salvation has been here from the beginning. God chose Abraham in order that "all the families of the earth shall be blessed" (Gen. 12:3). As a result of the death and resurrection of the true servant, Jesus Christ, the gospel has already been sent out to the nations, inviting all to be reconciled to God through faith (Matt. 28:18–20; Acts 1:8). We see Isaiah's promises fulfilled as a foreign eunuch is converted upon hearing the gospel preached from Isaiah 53 (Acts 8:26–38). This gospel continues to spread in our day, rescuing people from every tribe and language and people and nation (Mark 13:10; Rev. 5:9).

**PEACE.** The world is not the way it is supposed to be. Genesis 1–2 pictures a world of peace (Hebrew, *shalom*) and universal flourishing. There wasn't an ounce of tension between humanity and God, among humans, or anywhere else in the created world. But shalom was shattered because of sin. Humanity's relationship with God was severed (Gen. 3:23–24) and the peace with one another soon turned to shame, blame-shifting, and even murder (Gen. 3:7, 12–13; 4:8). Through Isaiah, God graciously proclaims reconciliation: "Peace, peace, to the far and to the near" (Isa. 57:19). The New Testament shows the dawn of this reality in Jesus Christ, who "came and preached peace to you who were far off and peace to those who were near" (Eph. 2:17). The hostility of Jews (the "near") and Gentiles (the "far off"), and any other hostility between peoples, was abolished at the cross, "for through him we both have access in one Spirit to the Father" (v. 18). Together we await the coming of the new creation, where we will dwell together with God in unending shalom.

## Theological Soundings

**FAITH AND WORKS.** "They seek me daily," God says, "and delight to know my ways" (Isa. 58:2). They "delight to draw near to God," but their obedience is merely external and their delight is insincere. Quarreling and oppression prove their religious devotion to be a farce (vv. 3–5). Jesus speaks of people who call him "Lord" and do many works in his name, yet whose disobedience demonstrates their lack of relationship with him (Matt. 7:21–23). Similarly, James reminds us that a non-working faith is a dead faith (James 2:17, 26). Throughout the Bible, we see that true faith always expresses itself in a life of love (Gal. 5:6). As Martin Luther put it, "we are saved by faith alone, but the faith that saves is never alone."

**RADICAL DEPRAVITY.** Isaiah 59:1–15 is unrelenting in its demonstration of humanity's sinfulness. The apostle Paul quotes portions of this text in Romans to support his conclusion that "None is righteous, no, not one" (Rom. 3:10; see 3:9–20). Since humanity's first sin, everyone who has lived is, as some theologians have called it, totally depraved.[3] This does not mean we are as bad as we can possibly be, for all people are created in God's image. Rather, total depravity means that every aspect of our lives is affected by sin. Thankfully, God's salvation is just as comprehensive, renewing the heart, mind, emotions, and will. Radical depravity is matched by radical grace.

> **Personal Implications**

Take time to reflect on the implications of Isaiah 56–59 for your own life today. Consider what you have learned that might lead you to praise God, repent of sin, and trust in his gracious promises. Make notes below on the personal implications for your walk with the Lord of (1) the *Gospel Glimpses*, (2) the *Whole-Bible Connections*, (3) the *Theological Soundings*, and (4) this passage as a whole.

## 1. Gospel Glimpses

## 2. Whole-Bible Connections

## 3. Theological Soundings

## 4. Isaiah 56–59

_____

_____

_____

_____

_____

_____

_____

_____

_____

_____

### As You Finish This Unit . . .

Take a moment now to ask for the Lord's blessing and help as you continue in this study of Isaiah. And take a moment also to look back through this unit of study, to reflect on some key things that the Lord may be teaching you—and perhaps to highlight and underline these things to review again in the future.

### Definitions

[1] **Peace** – In modern use, the absence of tension or conflict. In biblical use, a condition of well-being or wholeness that God grants his people, which also results in harmony with God and others.

[2] **Revival** – A renewed desire for spiritual things, brought about by the work of God.

[3] **Depravity** – The sinful condition of human nature apart from grace, whereby humans are inclined to serve their own wills and desires and reject God's rule.

# WEEK 11: THE RETURN OF THE LORD AND A NEW CREATION

Isaiah 60:1–66:24

Continuing from chapters 56–59, Isaiah writes about the time when exiles will return from Babylon and beyond. He looks to the distant future, speaking of the glory of God that will rise upon his people like a light in darkness (ch. 60) and an anointed one who will bring salvation and judgment (61:1–63:14). God will bring eternal judgment for the rebellious and eternal joy for his people, who will worship him in a new creation forever (63:15–66:24). This prophecy provides the motivation to humbly trust in God and await the fulfillment of his promises.

## The Big Picture

Isaiah 60–66 shows us that God will come in glory, bringing eternal judgment for the rebellious and joyful salvation in a new creation for all who trust him.

> ## Reflection and Discussion

Read through Isaiah 60–66, the passage for this week's study. Then review the following questions, taking notes on the final section of Isaiah's prophecy. (For further background, see the *ESV Study Bible*, pages 1349–1362; also available online at esv.org.)

### 1. The Anointed Preacher Announces Glory and Vengeance (60:1–63:7)

Isaiah 60 foresees all humanity uniting together in knowing the true God. God's glory will come to Jerusalem, displayed for his people as a light shining in darkness (v. 1; also vv. 19–20). What will the nations do at this time (vv. 3–9)? While Revelation shows us that this is still a future reality (note how Rev. 21:22–26 picks up Isa. 60:5, 11, 19–20), how does Matthew show that the fulfillment has already begun (read Matt. 2:9–11 with Isa. 60:1, 3, 6)?

How does the presence of the Spirit upon the anointed gospel preacher link him with other descriptions of a coming redeemer (compare Isa. 61:1 with 11:1–2; 42:1)? Review 9:6–7; 11:1–5; 42:1–7; and 52:13–53:12. What are the similarities between these descriptions?

Read Luke 4:16–21. What does Jesus' quotation of Isaiah 61:1–2 teach us about his identity and mission? Some interpreters have noted that Jesus stopped his quotation mid-sentence, leaving out, "and the day of vengeance of our God"

(Isa. 61:2). What does this imply about the difference between the primary agendas of his first and second comings?

As Isaiah 62 describes the transition of God's people from desolation to delight, God grants Jerusalem a new name, thus giving his people a new identity. How does the promise of a "new name" (v. 2), described in verses 4 and 12, summarize the restoration promises in this book?

What does the red color of the Messiah's garments indicate about what he will come to do (Isa. 63:1–6)? Read Revelation 19:11–16, noting the clear allusion to Isaiah 63:2–3 in Revelation 19:13, 15. How does this fill out our understanding of who the Messiah is and what he will do?

## 2. A Final Contrast: Humility unto Glory vs. Rebellion unto Destruction (63:7–66:24)

Isaiah 63:7–64:12 is an extended prayer. As Israel remembers God's love for them in the past (63:7–11a), they wonder why he seems aloof (vv. 11b–14). They plead with him to end their exile, just as he redeemed them at the exodus (63:15–64:3). In the following verses (64:4–12), what do we learn about

Israel and humanity's need for redemption? What do we learn about the God who redeems?

_____

_____

_____

_____

_____

_____

There is a clear contrast in Isaiah 65:1–16 between God's faithful remnant who seek him and those who forsake him. The remnant is repeatedly called God's "servants" (v. 8, 9, 13, 14, 15), implying that those who trust him are restored to their calling as God's servants in the world. How is their character and destiny contrasted throughout this passage with those who reject God?

_____

_____

_____

_____

_____

_____

Isaiah 65:17–25 describes a complete transformation of the cosmos, when God will "create new heavens and a new earth" (v. 17; see also 66:22). Isaiah uses imagery from his own time to paint a magnificent poetic picture of the new creation to come. What are specific ways Isaiah describes this coming world that go far beyond anything we have seen since sin entered the world? In light of Genesis 3:14–15, what is implied by Isaiah's promise, "dust shall be the serpent's food" (Isa. 65:25)?

_____

_____

_____

_____

_____

_____

The contrast between God's faithful remnant and the rebellious enemies continues into chapter 66. Isaiah is clear: people are in one of two categories, based not upon their ethnicity or merely external religious practices but upon their disposition toward God's words. How does Isaiah describe this contrast in 66:1–5? In practical terms, what would v. 2b look like for us today?

Isaiah ends with a vision of two contrasting eternal destinies. The first is of people from every nation worshiping God in his new creation (Isa. 66:19–23). How will their ingathering be accomplished? The second destiny is eternal destruction (66:15–18, 24). What is Isaiah seeking to accomplish in the readers by ending with these two divergent destinies?

Read through the following three sections on *Gospel Glimpses*, *Whole-Bible Connections*, and *Theological Soundings*. Then take time to consider the *Personal Implications* these sections may have for you.

## Gospel Glimpses

**LOOKING TO THE OVERLOOKED.** Some Israelites thought they could manipulate God—restricting his presence in the temple, putting him in their debt through religious practices (Isa. 66:3). But God will not be controlled, for "heaven is my throne," he declares, "and the earth is my footstool" (v. 1). Who, then, can hope to have him near? "This is the one to whom I will look," he says, "he who is humble and contrite in spirit and trembles at my word" (v. 2). God is present with the lowly. He looks at those whom the world overlooks. His gaze is set on those who know they are unworthy of it. Jesus did not come to save those who think they are righteous, but those who know they aren't. He came for any sinner who admits their need of him and humbly trembles at his word (Luke 1:48; 5:31; 7:36–50; 15:7). These are the ones whom he loves to bless.

ASTONISHING DELIGHT. One of the staggering realities of redemption is God's full-hearted delight in his people. As those who have rebelliously spurned him, we deserve only his eternal displeasure. Yet he promises not only to restore us but to delight in us with holy intensity, "as the bridegroom rejoices over the bride" (Isa. 62:5; also 65:19). Indeed, Zephaniah assures us that God, with all his might, "will exult over you with loud singing" (Zeph. 3:17). This incomprehensible love is not for the spiritual elite, with begrudging tolerance left over for the struggling. It is for anyone, even the worst of sinners, who brings his or her brokenness and asks for mercy.

> ## Whole-Bible Connections

RESTORED SERVANTHOOD. After reading Israel's mission to be God's "servant" in Isaiah 42:1–7, we read that they failed in this calling. Although they were to be a "light for the nations" that dwelt in darkness (vv. 6–7), Israel was as spiritually deaf and blind as the rest of the world (42:18–20). Because of this, an individual, righteous servant, a true Israel, would take up and fulfill their mission, bringing salvation to them and the nations through his sacrificial suffering and exaltation (Isaiah 49–53). As a result of this servant's redemptive work, God refers to his people once again as his "servants" (see 54:17; 56:6; 65:8–9, 13–15; 66:14). In other words, just as Isaiah was restored to God and then sent on mission (6:6–10), all who are likewise redeemed through the true servant's work are now restored to their original mission as God's servants. Since the true servant faithfully carried out their calling, those who are redeemed now look to him as their example of true servanthood. This shows us that the gospel carries with it not only forgiveness for our failure as servants but also restoration to this fundamental calling. Thus, Peter encourages us to look to Jesus, the suffering servant, as not only our Savior but also our example (1 Pet. 2:21–25; also Mark 10:42–45).

NEW CREATION. History is a story that stretches from creation to new creation. In the beginning, God created the heavens and the earth and pronounced them "very good" (Gen. 1:31). When sin entered the world, all of creation was "cursed" and "subjected to futility" (Gen. 3:17–18; Rom. 8:20). While the focus of redemption throughout the Bible is often on God's graciousness to forgive and reconcile individual human beings to himself, it is more broadly a plan for the entire cosmos. Isaiah promises that God will create "new heavens and a new earth" (65:17; 66:22). One day God will raise his people from the dead so that they will live with him, physically and forever, in a new creation. In fact, this has already begun through Jesus Christ. As the "firstborn" from the dead, he is the "beginning" of this new creation (Col. 1:18). Indeed, as those spiritually resurrected in Christ, his people are already "a new creation" (2 Cor. 5:17), awaiting the completion of their salvation in the coming new heavens and new earth (Rev. 21:1–5).

## Theological Soundings

**THE HOLY SPIRIT.** God saved Israel from Egyptian bondage and continually lavished them with love. Yet they rejected him. "They rebelled and grieved his Holy Spirit," Isaiah says (63:10; see vv. 11, 14). This description of God's response to his people's sin attributes personal characteristics to the Holy Spirit[1] (similarly, Eph. 4:30). Here is one of the Old Testament hints at the Trinity. The Bible presents the one God as eternally existing in three persons: Father, Son, and Holy Spirit.

**HELL.** Isaiah presents two contrasting eternal destinies. While those who trust in God will dwell with him in a new creation (Isa. 65:17; 66:22), those who rebel against him will face eternal judgment in hell. Using the imagery of the city dump, Isaiah says they will be slain, and "their worm shall not die, their fire shall not be quenched" (66:24). Jesus picks up this very imagery from Isaiah to describe the eternal suffering of hell (Mark 9:43–48). The only alternative to finding grace through Jesus Christ is a fearful expectation of eternal judgment. Through Isaiah, God graciously warns us to flee to him for rescue.

## Personal Implications

Take time to reflect on the implications of Isaiah 60–66 for your own life today. Consider what you have learned that might lead you to praise God, repent of sin, and trust in his gracious promises. Make notes below on the personal implications for your walk with the Lord of (1) the *Gospel Glimpses*, (2) the *Whole-Bible Connections*, (3) the *Theological Soundings*, and (4) this passage as a whole.

## 1. Gospel Glimpses

## 2. Whole-Bible Connections

## 3. Theological Soundings

## 4. Isaiah 60–66

> ### As You Finish This Unit . . .

Take a moment now to ask for the Lord's blessing and help as you continue in this study of Isaiah. And take a moment also to look back through this unit of study, to reflect on some key things that the Lord may be teaching you—and perhaps to highlight and underline these things to review again in the future.

### Definitions

[1] **The Holy Spirit** – One of the persons of the Trinity, and thus fully God. The Bible mentions several roles of the Holy Spirit, including convicting people of sin, bringing them to conversion, indwelling them and empowering them to live in righteousness and faithfulness, supporting them in times of trial, and enabling them to understand the Scriptures.

# WEEK 12: SUMMARY AND CONCLUSION

▲

We will conclude our study of Isaiah by summarizing the big picture of God's message through Isaiah as a whole. Then we will consider several questions in order to reflect on various Gospel Glimpses, Whole-Bible Connections, and Theological Soundings throughout the entire book.

## The Big Picture of Isaiah

Isaiah's message to his contemporaries remains relevant to all God's people until Christ returns. The prophecy has three main sections, each of which corresponds to a different historical setting.

The first section (chs. 1–39) is set against the background of Isaiah's own day in the eighth century BC. With the rising threat of the Assyrian empire, God's people were faced with a crisis of faith. Would they trust God or seek security in their own strategies for human rescue, turning to other nations for deliverance? Throughout this section, we learn that God will judge his own people, as well as people from all nations, for their deeply entrenched, arrogant, and rebellious ways. Yet God displays his gracious heart time and again as we hear surprising promises of restoration.

In the short-term, God will judge his people with exile in Babylon in the sixth century BC, which is the assumed background for the second section (chs. 40–55). God speaks into their brokenness with words of comfort. He promises restoration from physical bondage and exile through Cyrus (41–48), as well as restoration from spiritual bondage and exile through the servant (49–55).

While the physical restoration would be granted and the exiles would return home, God still announces the future fulfillment of his glorious promises in the final section (chs. 56–66). God redefines his people to include all who come to him in faith, from both Israel and all nations. To those who continue to rebel, he will bring everlasting judgment. But he will rejoice over all who trust him, granting everlasting joy in a new creation where they will worship him and enjoy him forever.

Read through the following three sections on *Gospel Glimpses, Whole-Bible Connections,* and *Theological Soundings.* Then take time to consider the *Personal Implications* these sections may have for you.

## Gospel Glimpses

Some have referred to Isaiah as the fifth gospel—"The Gospel according to Isaiah." Again and again, we have been confronted with God's just judgment of sinners, only to be suddenly surprised by an announcement of undeserved mercy. We have seen his promise not only to bring Israel out of their exile in Babylon, but to bring many from Israel and every nation out of their ultimate spiritual bondage to sin and exile from God's presence. God proclaims the good news that he will bring his kingdom and restore his people through the work of the suffering servant (Isa. 52:7–53:12).

Has Isaiah brought new clarity to your understanding of the gospel? How so?

--------

--------

--------

--------

--------

Were there any particular passages or themes in Isaiah that led you to have a fresh understanding and grasp of God's grace to us through Jesus?

--------

--------

--------

--------

--------

Isaiah gives us a panoramic picture of redemptive history, from creation to new creation, the curse to blessing, Exodus to New Exodus, Jerusalem to New Jerusalem, and sadness to singing. All of this turns upon the redemptive work of the servant, who takes the ultimate exile upon himself in order that those who trust him would be forgiven and restored to God (Isa. 52:13–53:12). We also find a multifaceted and captivating picture of this Messiah, Jesus Christ, who would come as an exalted king (9:6–7; 11:1–5), suffering servant (52:13–53:12), anointed preacher (61:1), and mighty conqueror (63:1–6).

How has this study of Isaiah filled out your understanding of the biblical story line of redemption?

Were there any themes emphasized in Isaiah that help you to deepen your grasp of the Bible's unity?

Have any passages or themes expanded your understanding of the redemption that Jesus provides, which he begun at his first coming and will consummate at his return?

What connections between Isaiah and the New Testament were new to you?

---------------------------------------

---------------------------------------

---------------------------------------

---------------------------------------

---------------------------------------

---------------------------------------

---------------------------------------

## ▶ Theological Soundings

Isaiah has much to contribute to Christian theology. Numerous doctrines and themes are developed, clarified, and reinforced throughout Isaiah, such as the grace and sovereignty of God, the sinfulness of humanity, the role and mission of Jesus Christ, and the eschatological kingdom of God.

Has your theology shifted in minor or major ways during the course of studying Isaiah? How so?

---------------------------------------

---------------------------------------

---------------------------------------

---------------------------------------

---------------------------------------

---------------------------------------

---------------------------------------

How has your understanding of the nature and character of God been deepened throughout this study?

---------------------------------------

---------------------------------------

---------------------------------------

---------------------------------------

---------------------------------------

---------------------------------------

---------------------------------------

---------------------------------------

94

What unique contributions does Isaiah make toward our understanding of who Jesus is and what he accomplished through his life, death, and resurrection?

What, specifically, does Isaiah teach us about the human condition and our need of redemption?

## Personal Implications

God wrote the book of Isaiah to transform us. As you reflect on Isaiah as a whole, what implications do you see for your life?

What implications for life flow from your reflections on the questions already asked in this week's study concerning Gospel Glimpses, Whole-Bible Connections, and Theological Soundings?

What have you learned in Isaiah that might lead you to praise God, turn away from sin, or trust more firmly in his promises?

## As You Finish Studying Isaiah . . .

We rejoice with you as you finish studying the book of Isaiah! May this study become part of your Christian walk of faith, day-by-day and week-by-week throughout all your life. Now we would greatly encourage you to study the Word of God on a week-by-week basis. To continue your study of the Bible, we would encourage you to consider other books in the *Knowing the Bible* series, and to visit www.knowingthebibleseries.org.

Lastly, take a moment to look back through this study. Review the notes that you have written, and the things that you have highlighted or underlined. Reflect again on the key themes that the Lord has been teaching you about himself and about his Word. May these things become a treasure for you throughout your life—which we pray will be true for you, in the name of the Father, and the Son, and the Holy Spirit. Amen.